W9-CUQ-950

Congratulat

Keep Gettin'
Geeky!

Gettin' Geeky

with

TWITTER

Build Your Business and
Manage Your Brand
with Today's Hottest
Social Media Tool

@GinaSchreck

Getting Geeky with Twitter: Build Your Business & Manage Your Brand with Today's Hottest Social Media Tool

@GinaSchreck

Published by
GG Publishing, Inc.
Littleton, CO 80125
www.GettinGeeky.com

Copyright © 2010 by GG Publishing, Inc. Littleton, Colorado

No part of this publication may be reproduced, stored in a retrieval system, or transmitted in any form or by any means, electronic, mechanical, photocopying, recording, scanning, written in sand on beaches in Figi, or otherwise, except as permitted under Sections 107 or 108 of the 1976 United States Copyright Act, without either the prior written permission of the Publisher, or authorization through payment of the appropriate person.

LIMIT OF LIABILITY/DISCLAIMER OF WARRANTY: The publisher and the author make no representations or warranties with respect to the accuracy or completeness of the contents of this work. The advice and strategies contained in this book may not be suitable for every situation, so consult a physician before you begin a strenuous exercise program including excessive Twittering. If professional assistance is required, the services of a competent professional person should be sought (this may be hard to find). Neither the publisher nor the author shall be liable for damages arising herefrom. The fact that an organization or Web site is referred to in this work as a citation or potential source of further information does not mean that the author or publisher endorses the organization. Readers should also be aware that Internet Web sites listed in this work may have changed or disappeared between when this work was written and when the reader finally got around to starting the book.

ISBN: 978-0-9763662-1-8
10 9 8 7 6 5 4 3 2 1

Who is Gina Schreck?

Gina Schreck is the co-founder and president of Synapse 3Di, LLC. The team at Synapse 3Di help individuals and organizations use today's technology to learn and to build their businesses. Gina hosts the popular web TV show *Gettin' Geeky* and speaks at conferences around the globe helping organizations use technology to improve learning, build business, and manage company and individual brands.

Gina has been using Twitter, Facebook, LinkedIn, virtual world platforms, YouTube, Skype, and just about every tech tool out there to connect and share big learning nuggets with the world. She is also a wife, mother of four, shoe-addict, coffee lover, and on most days, she wears the disguise of VIRTUAL GIRL (complete with cape)! As she tests the waters of new technology, Gina performs all of her own stunts and shares her experiences along the way.

Illustrations by the amazingly talented **Kevin Thorn** @Delanotho

Copy and Technical Editing by the amazing (and now geekier) **Julia Bate** @JuliaB8

This book is dedicated to the following people:

My patient family who has endured hours, days, weeks, and months of me attached to my laptop as I wrote and researched this book and twittered my fingers to the bone. My husband at least knew where to find me and what I was up to by logging into Twitter and reading my updates. I thank you for your patience, support, and endless material for me to tweet!

To all of my Twitter friends and acquaintances, you have kept me company while I traveled, made me laugh when I needed it, and taught me more than I thought possible. I tip my Twitter hat to you and express my deep gratitude!

Thank you,

@GinaSchreck

TOC

First Tweets Heard Around the World

"TRYING OUT TWITTER" **"Finally setting up Twitter...Hello?"** "Now to figure out what Twitter is all about." "Okay, I'm on Twitter···now what?" *"Hello World. Anyone out there?"* "Trying out Twitter today...Hmmm what now?" "I'm on Twitter now who will listen to me?" **"What to say, what to say?"** "I'M ON TWITTER. CAN YOU HEAR ME NOW?" "Hello! Any other coffee-serving, tweeting mannequins out there in the twitterverse?"

"I'm considering whether getting a Twitter account was a good idea or a bad idea" "So this is twittgr?" "New to this Twitter crap..now what?" **"I'm an official twit now at last..."** "Ok, here goes. My first *tweet*" "CREATED MY OWN TWITTER ;)" "Testing 123...test test"

These are some actual first tweets written by new twitterers. While they are funny to read, the common thread is: "I'm ready to connect, now who else is out there?"

It's probably the same thing Thomas Edison said when he plugged in his first telephone and picked up the receiver!

We've been connected ever since.

We have a need to speak out, to be heard. To successfully cohabitate in Twitter Town, remember to listen, engage, and connect.

INTWODUCTION

I'm not sure why most books have an introduction, but it could be so the writer has a runway or warm up place to get the ideas flowing. It could be so that you, the reader, can have a little background, or peek into the writer's thoughts before just diving into the content. But I wanted to wax eloquently for just a few sentences on the role Twitter is playing in our connected society.

It's interesting to know that this simple application has taken on a much bigger role in the way we communicate today than the founders, Evan Williams and Biz Stone, had ever imagined. Originally created as a simple way to tell friends and others what the user is working on or doing at the moment (like a blog, but in one sentence), Twitter has now morphed into a tool used for marketing, shaping company brands, connecting with experts, in addition to discovering what people are eating or watching on television. Twitter has allowed the users to innovate, and innovate they have.

Twitter is so much more than a fad, as some still perceive it. Twitter has changed our vocabulary, causing grown adults to use words like "tweet" and "retweet" without so much as cracking a smile. In November 2009, the Global Language Monitor named Twitter, its "Word of the Year." "Twitter represents a new form of social interaction, where all communication is reduced to 140 characters," said Paul JJ Payack, President of The Global Language Monitor. Microsoft also reported Twitter being the top search word for 2009 on its new search engine, Bing.

It has changed our tolerance for long, boring marketing brochures, rambling with company facts. Twitter is even helping people learn the art of brevity as they squeeze an important message into 140 characters.

In late 2007 I explored the concept of living in a society where we are no longer just "connected" but we are "hyperconnected." Because I am in a technology industry, I was probably more connected than most back then, but when I started examining those who were hyperconnected, even I was exhausted. More and more people fall into this category of hyperconnected.

I looked at how many applications and pieces of equipment the hyperconnected person typically used. Most used a cell phone, a laptop, a desktop computer, a Bluetooth device, a GPS, not to mention a land-line phone. As for applications to connect, folks were on Facebook, Myspace, LinkedIn, Plaxo, Hi5, Naymz, Slideshare, YouTube, Flickr, Digg, Delicious, Google Docs, old-fashioned e-mail, and of course Twitter—to name a few.

We are connected with more people than ever before, chatting, texting, instant messaging, tweeting, and writing on walls all over town. Most of us over the age of 35 have worried that our youth will not know how to hold a normal conversation when they enter the work place or that their thumbs will grow to be unusually large and they won't be able to open jars or brush their teeth. Come to find out, it is we "older folks" who are in danger. We are in danger of being passed by and disconnected.

In our fear to keep our kids from being hyperconnected, many of us have resisted crossing that digital divide and now find ourselves feeling left behind. Our work environments require us to work with team members and customers we have never met and who are scattered across the globe. We are expected to access information through social networks and other platforms, which require using the newest technologies. More families are using cell phones to stay connected. However these folks are talking on their cell phones far less often than they are texting and tweeting each other. I just wish they made bigger buttons on cell phones so I didn't have to wear glasses just to answer the messages that come via text instead of voice.

And what about the use of this technology in business? Customers don't have to wait in long lines or sit on hold in order to talk to a customer service agent when they have a problem. Like Tarzan, sending a call into the jungle to gather his tribe of animal friends to help him, you can simply send out a tweet and, within minutes, help is on its way. If help doesn't come in the form of a company representative tweeting you, it comes in the form of other twitterers who provide answers or pass along your dilemma to their tribes of people who probably have the answer for you.

Upset customers don't all go to the CONTACT US button on client websites anymore. Our society has learned that they can vent their frustrations in a tweet or even in a YouTube video. One upset customer wrote and posted music videos about an airline mishandling his luggage. You can believe he got a better response than contacting the customer complaint department! (Check out the songs *United Breaks Guitars* and *United Breaks Guitars II* by Dave Carroll on YouTube if you want proof of this one.)

DID YOU KNOW...

If your company doesn't have a blog or a Twitter account yet to engage customers in dialog when they are not happy, they will create their own place to chat about you, and you may not be invited into that conversation until the rest of the world has heard what a jerk you are. It's time to connect!

Is it right or wrong? Is this good for us or bad? Time will tell, but I see people using technology to learn, connect, market their businesses, and communicate with customers, and it sure beats many of the old ways of doing business. So whether you are hyperconnected or just dipping your toe into the virtual waters of an ever-growing stream of conversation, let's explore ways to use today's technology to make meaningful connections and learn BIG things.

Twapter 1

What is Twitter & Why Should You Be Tweeting?

Twapter 1: What is Twitter & Why Should You Be Tweeting?

There are more books about Twitter on Amazon than there are about Rocket Science or Brain Surgery...or was it there are more books about Twitter than there are about Rocket Surgery? (At the time of this writing, if you type "Twitter" into Amazon BOOK SEARCH, you can choose from over 18,000 entries. Type in "Rocket Science" and you find slightly over 9,700.) As you first dive into the Twitter nest, you may feel like this is rocket science, but stick with it and soon you will find it is as easy as pie. (There are over 371,000 books about pies!)

Either way, there are plenty of resources out there to learn to use this social media tool, but many of them focus on how to get 50,000 followers in two weeks to make thousands of dollars. I believe that kind of mindset that keeps many people away from Twitter. Why do I want one more tool that allows people to scream, "Buy! Buy! Buy!" in my face?

This book offers practical tips on using to Twitter to build your business, manage your brand, and connect with great people—customers, potential customers, and unfamiliar people with similar interests—that you can learn lots from.

What this is NOT:

This is not a book that will teach you how to get thousands of followers overnight, and yet you will learn how to grow your network to include thousands of followers, if that is what you choose. Developing a relevant network takes some time.

This is not a book that will teach you how to make thousands of dollars on Twitter in the first week, but you will connect with potential customers and contacts that can help you grow your business resulting in potentially thousands of dollars, and it won't be a scam.

So, if that was the kind of book you were looking for, buy this one anyway and give it to one of your friends. You can search on Amazon for one of those *other* books.

BUT...

What if you had a tool that fed you the latest information on your area of expertise *before* a blog or article was written about it? What if you could connect with experts and potential business contacts, learning bits of information about them *without* cold calling, adding them to your e-zine list, or sending a LinkedIn or Facebook contact request?

Twitter is that tool! Whether you are intrigued and looking to jump into the Twitter stream or you are still not sure what value can come from a bunch of strangers sharing a couple of sentences with one another like one big cocktail party, this book will provide insight, tips, and techniques to help you join the social network, learn more than you thought you would, and even build your business.

So what exactly is Twitter? It is a social networking phenom, combining aspects of social media with micro-blogging. Twitter is used to deliver byte-sized pieces of information to anyone who is following those updates. (Think "tribes.") It is like sending a text message, but instead of sending it to just one person, you are broadcasting it to everyone who has chosen to follow you.

DID YOU KNOW...

Google and other search engines are always listening. Every 140 character tweet is a fully indexed webpage, so with a little strategic focus and keyword application, your tweets will really work for you!

Because Twitter allows us to send short "micro-blog" updates as often as we'd like, people will mix in more personal information than they might in a regular blog, and this allows you to peek into their personal life and find those commonalities that can actually begin a relationship. Twitter is what goes on between blog posts and email.

By finding and following experts, favorite bloggers, authors, and business leaders, Twitter becomes a valuable tool for learning, and when you engage customers and potential customers in conversation, you gain information to improve and build your business.

Marketing is no longer the greatest skill needed within a company; conversing is. Old marketing is when you push information out to a target market through brochures, direct mail, broadcasting, and other forms of advertising. It's material that you think is fabulous but often the recipients call it "junk mail." Old marketing is you standing on the corner with your marketing material, yelling, "*Buy my stuff! Work with me—I'm the best!*" Most people walk past trying hard to avoid eye contact.

New marketing is all about engaging people in conversations, providing helpful information and resources for them. In this type of approach, you listen more than you speak, learning what your customers are interested in and what they need. New marketing draws people to you, without having to yell or hand them anything, unless, of course, they ask you for it.

On the new marketing corner, people, in a sense, are standing around you drinking coffee and writing your contact information down for themselves and for their friends.

Twitter is the power tool today that allows you to engage, listen and even share a cup of coffee with a new friend, as you look for ways to work together. Twitter can let you in on conversations with people you may never have come in contact with otherwise. Those who don't get it are still licking stamps to put on their marketing material and heading down to the corner mailbox.

Thoughts & Notes

Twapter 2

Building the Nest: Going Beyond Just Signing Up!

Twapter 2: Building the Nest: Going Beyond Just Signing Up!

This is a critical first step. Many people make the mistake of signing up for Twitter without building their nest properly. The pieces in your nest include creating a keyword-rich profile in 160 characters, loading your headshots, and adding links to your website or blog.

Okay let's jump off the edge of the nest and start flying. To begin, go to www.Twitter.com and click on the SIGN UP NOW button. (*figure* 2.1)

Figure 2.1

IMPORTANT: I believe it is ideal is to grab your name (first & last) for your Twitter handle, but if that is not available, or if that is too long, choose something that makes it easy for people to find you. Just like trying to snag the URL for a website, many people got in early and took celebrity names (just look at how many combinations of Michael Jackson, Brittany Spears, or any other famous names there are) or common names and they just sit on them. They're called **name squatters.** I'm not exactly sure what their motive is. Some take a famous name and just cause trouble, posting weird information as if they were that person, and some hope that they can sell the account back to the famous person for a pretty penny! So if your name is taken, you may have to settle for your second or third choices.

Don't worry if you change your mind later, Twitter allows you to go back and change your user name. If you use something creative or different from your real name for your user name, be sure to put your full name in the first field so folks can find you using search or it can defeat your purpose on Twitter.

The first field asks for your full name. This is what people will see when they go to your Twitter page or hover over your screen name. The second field is your user name, the "Twitter-handle" that people use to send you Tweets. (*figure* 2.2) These two can be the same thing or your user name may be a nickname. Because each tweet is only 140 characters, a long user name can get in the way. **SHORT is SWEET.** Aim for 10 letters or fewer. The maximum number of characters allowed for a user name is 15, so choose wisely.

Once you are finished with this step, click the CREATE MY ACCOUNT button, Twitter will wave its magic tail feathers, and your account will be created.

You will see a message asking if you want to look for people to connect through your email networks. I recommend skipping this step, as we will look at how to find the right people to follow a little bit later in **Twapter 8.**

For now let's finish building your nest~

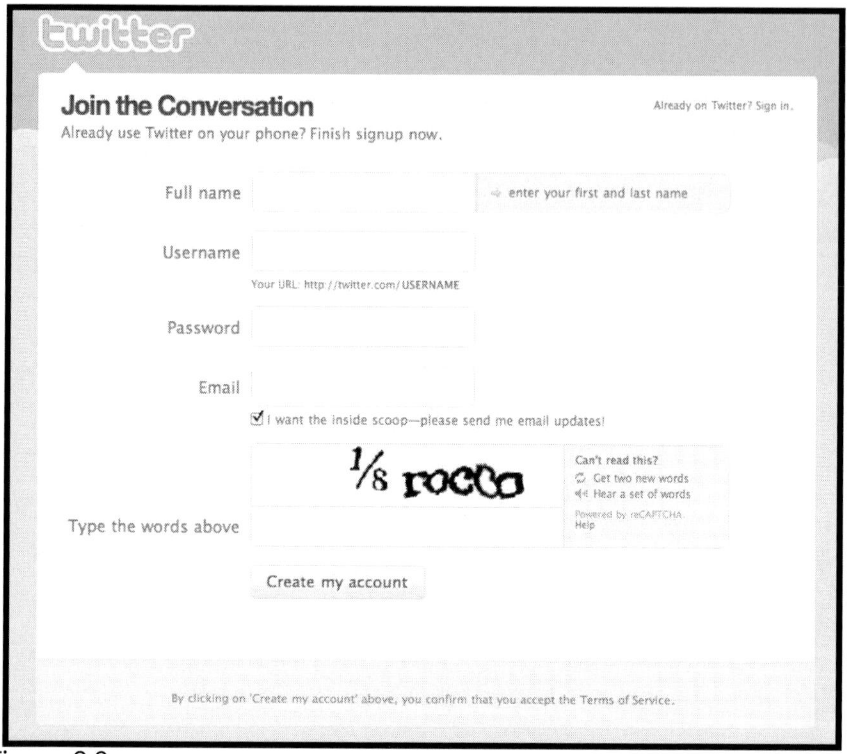

Figure 2.2

Let's go through the set up tabs.

You have your real name and username (which may be the same thing) filled out. Your email should also be listed here, showing you where email notices will go. Your email will not be displayed to the public. Select your time zone and add a website link. The website link is important to point people to another location to find out more information about you and your business. You can point folks to a blog, a website, or if you don't yet have either of those, add your Facebook or LinkedIn URL here.

In the ONE LINE BIO box, you have **160 characters** (that includes spaces and punctuation) to describe who you are, your interests, or simply fill it with key words that will help people find you and connect. Try and use as many of those characters as possible. (*figure* 2.3)

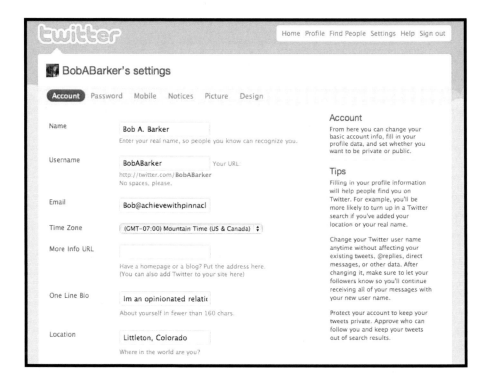

Figure 2.3

You can tweak your profile as often as you'd like. Play around with it and see which keywords attract the most relevant followers.

Under location, you can put your city, state or make a sarcastic statement such as "Everywhere you want to be." People do use location as a search term when wanting to connect with folks in a specific geographical location, so depending upon how you will be using Twitter, you may or may not want to be very specific here.

Examples of good profile information include:

"VP in Pharmaceutical & Healthcare industry. Father of 5 boys & a dog. Coffee and potato chip addict, interested in all things Italian and related to great food." (159 characters)

"Blogger, truck driver & animal enthusiast. Mother to 7 dogs, 4 snakes & 16 parrots. I live alone (I wonder why) and I'm always in search of peace and quiet." (156 characters)

 "Speaker, author, Geeky Girl, LOVER of SHOES, www.GettinGeeky.com host, Helping people w/BYTE-sized learning thru live events, Second Life, videos, podcsts & more" (This is a brilliant 160 characters...and ... wait! This is MY PROFILE!)

After the location setting you will see Twitter's Geotagging option. (figure 2.4)

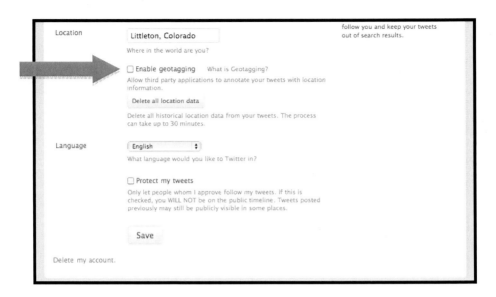

Figure 2.4

Twitter's Geotagging feature allows users to Geotag their tweets with their **exact location** and provide more context to users about their surroundings. This is an "opt-in" feature and I suggest you use caution. While it can be useful when trying to coordinate a "Tweet Up" (meeting of several Twitter users) or to send out conference and event information, this feature is not for every situation. If you are hiking through the Himalayan Mountains and want to allow folks to follow you on your trek, this would be a good use for Geotagging, but understand it can be risky to let the world know exactly where you are… on a regular basis. Read more about Twitter's Geotagging feature by clicking on "What is Geotagging?" next to the enable box.

Geotagging is the process of adding geographical identification metadata to various media such as photographs, video, websites, or RSS feeds and is a form of geospatial metadata. These data usually consist of latitude and longitude coordinates, though they can also include altitude, bearing, accuracy data, and place names. (from Wikipedia: http://en.wikipedia.org/wiki/Geotag)

After reading that cautionary tale about Geotagging, you may be tempted to now check the box, "Protect my Tweets," (figure 2.5) but hold on.

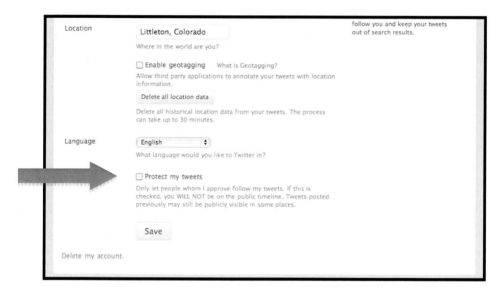

Figure 2.5

There are some organizations that use Twitter to communicate information internally, to employees or members of an association and they do not want that information going out to the world. If this is how you are using Twitter, you will want to check this box and then communicate to your team that they must request to connect and that they will agree not to "retweet" or forward information sent through this account, out to their other Twitter connections.

Most people want the world to be able to receive their updates and posts, so checking this box will greatly affect that goal. By checking this box, your Twitter account becomes like your LinkedIn or Facebook profile, in that folks have to ask for your permission to connect and wait for your response. If you are using Twitter as a marketing or public relations tool, you **DO NOT** want this box checked. Enough said.

Setting Up Your Mobile Device

The MOBILE tab allows you to connect your cell phone number so that you can send tweets from your mobile phone as an SMS text message (regular text message charges from your cell provider may apply).

DID YOU KNOW? SMS stands for Simple Message Service, which refers to simple text being sent through your cell phone. MMS stands for Multimedia Message Service, which is how it is sent when you add a photo or video to a text message!

Why, you might ask, would you want to text from your cell phone? Well, there are times you are out and something happens that is "tweet-worthy." There are also times you are at a conference or event and you will want to share that experience with others in Twitter Town. If your cell phone is set up to send a tweet now and then, you will be able to capture and share the moment when it strikes your fancy!

On your mobile, set up a contact named Twitter and put the code that is listed for your country (*figure* 2.6) as the number to send your tweets to. You do not have to receive your tweets on your phone. In fact, I suggest that you don't receive tweets on your mobile phone, because your cell phone will chime incessantly, not to mention the fact that, if you do not have unlimited text messaging, you could easily rack up hundreds of dollars on your cell phone bill. If you have unlimited text messaging, you are covered here, but you still probably don't want that many text messages coming into your phone.

In **Twapter 16** you can gather some information about using a mobile app that can be used to tweet, saving your SMS text messaging.

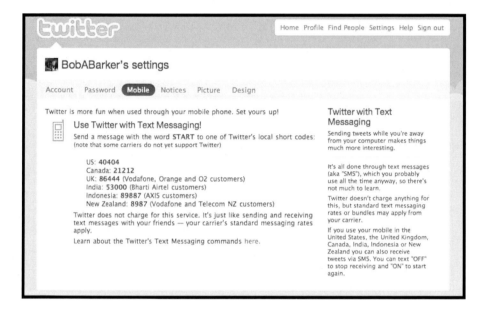

Figure 2.6

The default setting on Twitter will **not** have the tweets of those you are following come to your cell phone. But, if there **are** one or two people that you want to follow when you are away from your computer, you can click on their individual profiles and under their photos, you will see a check mark showing you are following them. Next to the word "Following" you will see a small gray cell phone icon. If you would like this person's updates coming to your phone, click on the icon and it will turn green, letting you know that the updates for this particular person will now be sent to your cell phone via SMS text. (*figure* 2.7) You can make these changes any time.

Figure 2.7

If the person is too chatty or you simply get tired of the messages showing up on your cell phone, you can change this back. Just go back to the person's profile and click on the green cell phone icon to turn it gray again.

Keeping You Informed

The NOTICES tab (*figure* 2.8) allows you to select whether you will receive an email notifying you when someone new is following your updates or if someone has sent you a direct message. You can also sign on to receive any Twitter news they decide to send out.

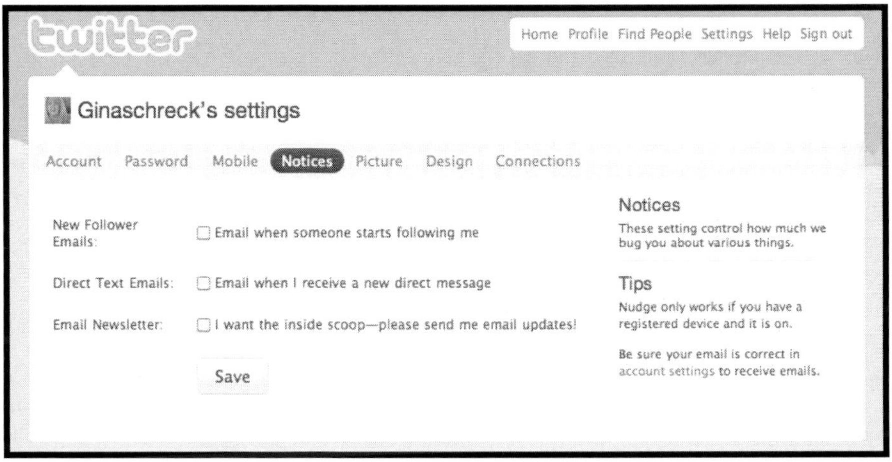

Figure 2.8

In the beginning, you may want to receive an email when someone new is following your updates so you can click the link that takes you to his/her profile, to see if you want to follow that person's updates. If the notifications become too much, simply go back into the settings and uncheck that box.

I recommend, at least in the beginning, you keep the box checked to receive an email notification when someone sends you a direct message, since those are usually more important tweets. Once you are in the habit of logging into Twitter daily and checking to see if you have any new followers and direct messages, this feature can be dropped.

Thoughts & Notes

Twapter 3

Say Tweese! Choosing a Photo & Creating an Avatar to Represent Each Tweet

Twapter 3: Say Tweese! Choosing a Photo & Creating an Avatar to Represent Each Tweet

With so many social networking sites and bits of information coming at us, getting recognized and standing out to your customers, contacts, and even your friends and family is getting harder and harder. A great avatar will help you stand out, get recognized, and be memorable.

Note: An avatar is a digital representation of you, be it a photo, a caricature, or a computerized character resembling you. Avatar, headshot, or profile picture are all simply "mugshots!"

In my opinion, the ideal is to use the same avatar (or one that is very similar) for all of your social sites—Twitter, Facebook, LinkedIn, Flickr, SlideShare, etc. Your avatar will brand you. People may not remember your name but they will recognize your face or picture. I would also caution you not to change your photos too often—unless of course it has been several years since you updated your photo, and you now look like the grandparent of your old self.

What makes a great avatar? Remember, an avatar image helps people connect with you. Not your dog, not your car, but you...your face. There are a few (very few) who can pull off using a picture of an animal or object, but that is their brand, and they tweet from the angle of that brand.

Regardless of the type of business you are in, social networking sites are about social networking. That implies a personal connection, but not too personal. Some people take pictures while wearing practically nothing and expect to get followers...well they'll get followers, just not ones most people want.

You do not need a professional photographer or a glamour shot look. You can take a great picture using your computer or have someone snap a photo of you with a digital camera. Crop a headshot from a photo showing you smiling, laughing, or, if you are always scowling, grab that shot.

Your avatar should show your personality and stand out. Even though some of these folks have already changed their pictures, I picked these out as some of my favorites and here is why I like them:

1   2   3   4

1-@Macker 's pic stands out because he is NOT smiling. Perhaps this is his sulking, pouty, or worn out pastor look.

2-@LordMattBorg is as unique as his photo. When you see his pic pop up, you know it will be something...uh... let's just say it will be like his photo!

3- @NameTagScott has a photo that is his brand. FUN!

4- @NeilMcKenzPhoto has a photo that does break my rule of not showing his face, but it is unique and clearly shows you everything he probably wants you to know about him.

5   6   7   8

5- @LinkedInExpert has a FABULOUS smile and you feel happy just seeing her picture not to mention the great content Viveka (her real name) provides!

6- @Poinky stands out for obvious reasons and everywhere you see him...he's green. (As a "Schreck," I like green!)

7- @Quinnovator has such a friendly face and is just as friendly and smart in person.

8- @MelissaWrites shows another great smile in a clear close up photo.

9   10   11   12

9- @Linnetwoods and her fun hat always grabs my attention. She is a great connector and has fun contests she hosts through Twitter, so this avatar matches her online persona perfectly!

10- @ChrisVoss has a great close up shot. You also get the feeling from his picture that he has a fun personality to go along with the great social media content he provides.

11- @JennFor uses her Second Life avatar headshot which I love since she does so much in the immersive learning environment. The interesting thing is she looks just like her avatar!

12- @LiveYourBrand (Lethia Owens) Her photo is eye-catching. Fabulous smile, close up headshot, and striking colors to pop out and call to you.

 13    14

13- @LilPecan is one of the few animal avatars that works for me. She's witty and smart, besides the fact that she sings scat and has a face that you just love to see on your Twitter feed.

14- @Forces2 is a little warped squirrel that spews out hilarious and cynical comments and one-liners. (I think he channels the comedian Steven Wright at times!)

The absolute worst avatar you can have is no avatar at all. DO NOT let Twitter give you the default silhouette of blandness.

 Who are you?

This default avatar tells the world you started tweeting before you were ready or that you got really frustrated trying to load a picture and gave up. It's kind of like people who shave, brush their teeth, or put on make-up while driving to work. Stay home and finish getting ready before you walk out the door. Don't start following people until you are fully dressed.

Some people use a logo or picture of the book they have just written, but they are missing the point. Twitter involves small conversations.

Conversations are between people. Engage with people and they will want to find out more about you and what you are doing. You can link to your books or products in Tweets, and people will click on you more often if they know and like you already.

If you are using Twitter to manage your corporate brand and want to engage customers with your brand, then a logo is fine, but the conversations will be different. I suggest that companies show a picture of who is tweeting on their behalf. If there are several people, add initials or names with the tweets. Down the left side of the profile page, list who is tweeting for this organization so people can feel as if they are getting to know the people behind the brand. There are tools such as CoTweet or Hootsuite, to help you with this and you can find out more information on them in **Twapter 16**. For some corporate examples, check out @ComcastCares, @HyattConcierge, @Rubbermaid, or @Starbucks. They do a good job of interacting with customers, providing content that is packed with helpful tips or interesting trivia, and if you have a problem with their brand, they are just a tweet away, ready to help.

How do you load your photo?

For a profile picture there is a maximum size of 700k. For a background image there is a maximum size of 800k. Images must be in a JPG, GIF, or PNG format.

Images don't need to have certain dimensions; however, the profile picture will be cropped to square if the original is not. I recommend uploading an image that is below 700k and also as close to square as possible. Here are the steps to follow. (See *figure* 3.1)

1. **Click SETTINGS**
2. **Click on the PICTURE tab**
3. **Click on the CHOOSE FILE button to locate your photo on your computer**
4. **Once it shows that the file is there, click SAVE (only once)**
5. **Now click back on your link to HOME view**

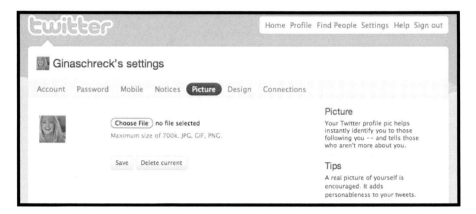

Figure 3.1

Twapter 4

How Stella Got Her Twitter Back

Twapter 4: How Stella Got Her Twitter Back

The backgrounds on Twitter have become as unique as the people behind the tweet. You can change your background by selecting the DESIGN tab. Now you may choose to leave the default Twitter background, and many people live a long, happy Twitter life with that design. Most people, when they learn they can change the background, want to express themselves and show their personality here.

There are several semi-custom backgrounds you can choose from on the Twitter DESIGN tab (*figure* 4.1), or you can upload a completely custom look, even matching your website or blog, by uploading a JPG picture. You can use a photo or other graphic and alter it using MS Paint, Photoshop, or even create your background in PowerPoint, and then save it as a JPG. Simply create your slide and go up to FILE, click SAVE AS in PowerPoint, select JPG, and then upload it on the DESIGN page.

Figure 4.1

Since Twitter only gives you space for 160 characters to describe yourself and your business, a custom background can be a great place to put a bit more information about you and list other contact information such as your Facebook page, LinkedIn profile, or blog. Look at the backgrounds on some Twitter pages of other peeps to note what you do and don't like. You have a block of space on the left side of your Twitter feed and another small strip of space on the right.

Tips for creating your own custom background

Keep in mind that the size and resolution of a person's screen will determine how much of your background is seen. Lower resolution, 800 X 600 for instance, will display differently than a higher resolution, 2048 X 1536, so play around with the photo size and see which displays your graphic best for MOST screen sizes. Here are the standard measures used by most Twitter background designers.

> Image Width: 1255 pixels
> Image Height: 555 pixels
> Left Graphic Width: 245 pixels
> Right Graphic Width: 250 pixels

Many people use a photo-editing program such as Photoshop to create their Twitter background, but if that seems too technical for you, and you still want more than the semi-custom Twitter options, you can check out www.Twitbacks.com, www.TwitterBackgrounds.com, or www.Twitterbacks.com to choose from hundreds of fun templates. These sites offer some free templates and complete custom designs for a fee.

Twapter 5

Important Twicks of the Twade: How to Start Tweeting

Twapter 5: Important Twicks of the Twade: How to Start Tweeting

Most updates or tweets will be messages you intend to send out to the world, or at least to those following your updates. The question Twitter asks is, "What's happening?" I really wish it asked something like, "What do you have to say that is interesting or helpful?" But it doesn't, and it really doesn't matter what the question is. It is your reply that is most important.

There are some variations of your tweets that are crucial to understand before you open your mouth to tweet. You don't want to send private information out to everyone, if it was only intended for one specific person. Conversely, you don't necessarily want to send a private message to someone if it could be interesting or helpful to the world. So let's look at the 4 types of Tweets:

1. **REGULAR UPDATES**

   An update is simply a message, question, quote, witty observation, helpful tip, resourceful link, or just about anything else you can squeeze into 140 characters. This is a thought or message coming from you and going out to all who follow your updates. There is nothing special you have to do. You simply write your tweet in the update box and hit UPDATE. (figure 5.1)

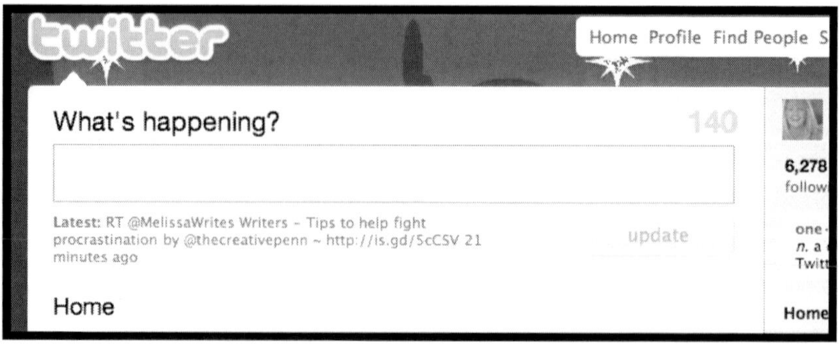

Figure 5.1

2. DIRECT MESSAGES

These are private messages sent to one person. No one else will see a direct message, and it will not be posted on your string of tweets for anyone else's viewing pleasure.

Let's say you wanted to send a tweet directly to a contact asking that person to call you and you need to put your cell number in the tweet. For example: On my way-need directions. Call my cell 303-555-5555.

You DO NOT want this going out to the world... no matter how lonely you are!

So, to send it direct, or private, you simply type a "D" in front of the person's Twitter name to ensure it goes directly to that person and no one else. You do NOT need the @ symbol before their name when sending a direct message. You would type it like this:

D Ginaschreck Here's my cell number 303-555-5555. I'm on my way-call me

IMPORTANT: If you do not see the "D" in front of the person's name, it is NOT in direct mode and will go out to everyone. This happened to a friend, who sent a somewhat nasty note, and instead of "D" he had "@" in front of the message. The note went to everyone! At least he got the attention quickly of the person he needed to hear from.

As soon as you type the letter "d" followed by a space, and it does not matter whether it is upper or lower case, you will see the message above change from "What's happening?" to "Direct Message." (*figure* 5.2)

Figure 5.2

Until you become more familiar with Twitter or use a tool like **TweetDeck, Seesmic,** or one of the other third-party tools that allows you to quickly see when you have a message, you will need to be sure and check your Direct Messages inbox often in case someone has sent you a direct message and is waiting for a reply.

The best way to do this is to use a tool like **TweetDeck** (www.TweetDeck.com) which pulls all direct messages into a column for you to see quickly and easily. You can learn more about this in **Twapter 16.**

As mentioned in **Twapter 2**, click on the SETTINGS link (at the top right), under the NOTICES tab, you may want to check the box that says, "Email when I receive a new direct message." (*figure 5.3*) You can change this later when you are in the habit of checking in with your peeps daily.

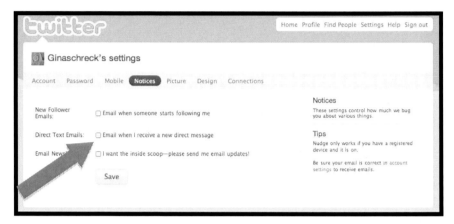

Figure 5.3

3. THE REPLY

A reply is a message that is going to everyone following your updates, but it provides context by beginning the reply with someone's Twitter name. For example: @Ginaschreck I love that song too! Without the "@username" in the beginning, the reply doesn't make sense. By starting with it...well, it's still a bit confusing, but you do have a little context—it tells that this tweet is in reply to something the named person said.

To reply to someone's tweet, simply move your cursor to the right of that tweet and click on the REPLY button, right beside the RETWEET button. When you click on the REPLY button, your message box changes again, from "What's happening?" to "Reply to username." (*figure 5.4*)

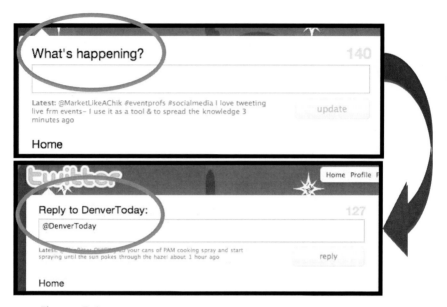

Figure 5.4

4. RETWEETS

Retweeting is like forwarding an email message. You pass along the content as well as showing where it originated. The retweet wasn't originally built into the Twitter platform and yet it has become one of the most popular features. Twitter users can share great content they receive with those following their updates, allowing that great content to become more viral. If your tweets get retweeted or forwarded, it multiplies the reach of your message and can build your Twitter reputation.

The key to successful retweeting, is fitting it all in 140 characters, because when you forward the message, it keeps the original person's Twitter username in the space. You usually have to do some editing to reduce the number of characters, which is perfectly acceptable, but gets a little tricky.

There are a few ways to retweet a message. You can select

the retweet symbol on the Twitter home page by hovering over the bottom right area of the specific tweet. (*figure* 5.5)

Quinnovator RT @MindWareToys: How kids want to learn - new research emerges: http://bit.ly/6rYYyj
less than 20 seconds ago from TweetDeck
Reply
Retweet

Figure 5.5

When you select RETWEET from here, it will send the entire message, along with the person's name, but will not allow you to add anything to the tweet or shorten it if it was too long to fit in the 140-character space. The RETWEET symbol will show in front of the update. (*figure* 5.6)

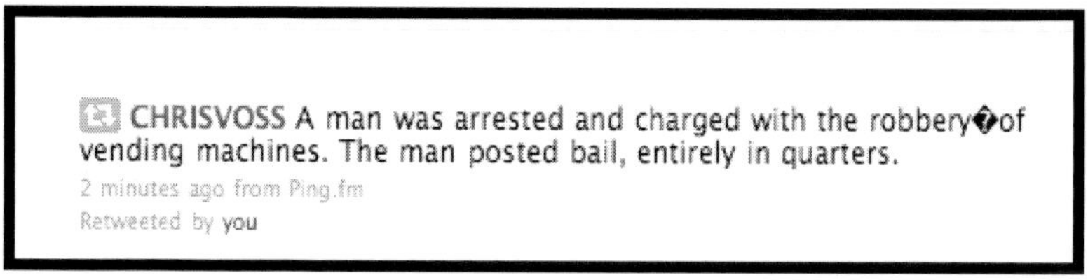
CHRISVOSS A man was arrested and charged with the robbery�of vending machines. The man posted bail, entirely in quarters.
2 minutes ago from Ping.fm
Retweeted by you

Figure 5.6

If you prefer, you can copy and paste the entire message (including the reference of who sent it) into the update bar. In front of the entire message put "RT" and then a space (*figure* 5.7). Some put the source at the end, but this can be confusing and lead to plagiarism if the originator's name gets left off. (*figure* 5.8) This allows you to make a comment at the end of the post letting your followers know your thoughts on the tweet.

Figure 5.7

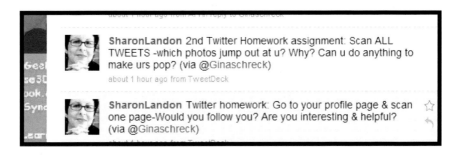

Figure 5.8

You want to work at getting your messages retweeted, so that you multiply the power of your reach. Remember, even if you only have 5 people following you, but those 5 people each have 5,000, your influence is greater than you think, so put great content out that gets retweeted.

When crafting a "tweet-worthy" message, plan ahead, and see if you can squeeze the message into **120 characters.** This makes it easier for folks to retweet it, since they have to fit your Twitter handle (username) along with "RT" in front of the actual message. Put thought into your tweets before hitting send and you will be rewarded.

Thoughts & Notes

_____

_____

_____

_____

_____

_____

_____

_____

_____

_____

_____

_____

_____

_____

Twitter Tip: Check out www.Twinfluence.com to get an idea of the kind of Twinfluence you have. Twinfluence is a simple tool for measuring the combined influence of twitterers and their followers, with a few social network statistics thrown in as bonus.

Another great site to check out retweeters and the hottest topics is http://Retweetist.com .

Twapter 6

Tweet Like Donny & Marie! Mixing Business with Personal

Twapter 6: Tweet like Donny and Marie! Mixing Business with Personal

Do you remember the *Donny and Marie Show*? No, not *Dancing with the Stars*. Donny and Marie Osmond performed in a variety show back in the late '70s. They began each show singing, "I'm a little bit country. I'm a little bit rock n roll!" Perhaps that is a bad analogy for this section, and it just brought back scary images of polyester bellbottoms and really bad hair, but Donny and Marie have great teeth!

Let's try another analogy. Twitter is like a great meal. You have the main course, but that alone is not what makes the meal great. You need fabulous appetizers and wonderful sides, and of course something a little sweet at the end. Successful Twitterers have learned to mix business with enough personal comments to season and sweeten the connections.

If you are on Twitter to simply sell people on your webinar series, or to get people to buy your diet pills or books, followers will quickly grow tired of your pitch and "unfollow" you. Or at least tune you out.

If you are on Twitter just for the social connections, your "sweetness" will soon give some people a toothache. It is like when an unemployed friend calls you 87 times at work to tell you what she discovered at the local coffee shop that morning and about the flowers she is going to plant when it gets a little warmer outside, and then moves on to discussions about a dinner party and who is invited which is causing drama among…. (Oh sorry, that was a conversation I just had with my unemployed friend!) You start checking caller ID before answering. Twitter is no different.

A question I get every time I speak on this topic is, "What's the percentage of personal versus business that I should use?" This will be different for each person, but just remember you are involved in short conversations about things that interest you. Imagine that we work together. How much of our day would be spent sharing pertinent information and how much water-cooler chat would we have? It is similar on Twitter.

Don't be afraid to let people get to know you, but if you start sharing too much information and telling us how often you clip your toenails, we will be requesting a transfer pretty fast!

Twapter 7

Be Intweresting, Be Helpful, or Shut Your Beak!

Twapter 7: Be Intweresting, Be Helpful, or Shut Your Beak!

With thousands of people sending thousands of tweets into Twitter Town every minute, you'd better be interesting if you want to be heard. Twitter Town rewards captivating, relevant comments.

Too many people waste time blathering about what they ate or posting what time they woke up and what they are doing every minute of their day. That is not only NOT engaging or helpful, but no one cares or wants to see that come across the screen. Now, if you tell me where you ate a great sandwich and included a link to the restaurant, at least you are being helpful. If you are watching TV, at least share the name of the show or something that I can engage with, such as "Watching *Biggest Loser* and eating ice cream...Is that wrong?"

Twitter helps us become better writers, if we work at it. It is possible to be helpful, witty, and concise, but you will have to put forth some effort. The good news is when you do put forth a wee bit of effort, the payoff can be huge. Since most tweets are mundane, yours can stand out in the flock. Here are some examples and tips:

BORING: Eating a piece of cake

FUN: Staring longingly at each other, the last piece of cake & I realize we were meant to be together!

NOT HELPFUL: (and rather braggadocios) found great shoes today on sale

HELPFUL: Got AWESOME shoes today 50% off- Get yours quick http://greatshoes.com

BORING & NOT HELPFUL: National Speaker's Association meet in Phoenix for convention.

FUN & HELPFUL: What happens when 1000 speakers w Hot Air gather where its already HOT? NSA taking Global Wrming to new levels! http://NSASpeaker.org

MUNDANE: Robert Frost "2 roads diverge in a wood, I took the one less traveled & that has made all the difference."

CLEVER: 2 roads diverge in woods- Robert Frost took the one less traveled- I'm stuck in traffic!

SAPPY: The sun will come out tomorrow~ Annie

SNAPPY The sun will come out tomorrow-PUT ON YOUR SUNSCREEN!

MORE TIPS:

- Show us your personality. People don't want to read just facts scrolling across the screen like a news report (unless of course unless you are @CNN or @FOXNEWS, etc.). We want to get to know you.

- Provide tips that showcase your expertise. If you are a relationship expert, write a tip each day that helps me with my relationships. "Leave a sticky note for your beloved and draw a stick figure to illustrate your love." If you are a fitness guru, give me a tip I can do while sitting at my desk to start feeling the burn.

- Provide details so peeps can engage with you. "Listening to my favorite tunes" is not interesting, but if you tell us which tunes you are listening to, we can engage with you, telling you how much we LOVE Sting and Phil Collins too.

- Be thought provoking. "If Mark Twain or Marie Antoinette were on Twitter, what would they tweet?" This can evoke great tweet responses.

- Survey the crowd. Ask a question that will get people responding, such as "What is the first thing you do when you check into a hotel? Share your answers."

- Don't give us TMI (too much information)! Okay, I know I just said to give us details, but when it comes to your private life or disgusting bodily functions or "malfunctions" we just don't need to know!

- Don't tell us how much you hate your boss, your ex, your mother, or co-worker. Save that for your therapy session and remember that every tweet is a fully indexed and archived forever webpage. It can be found and used against you. Even if you delete the tweet after sobering up and coming to your senses, it has been sent to your followers who may have retweeted it, replied to it, or copied and pasted it into a legal document that can and will be used against you in a court of law. You will be held accountable for your words, actions, and tweets, so think before you hit SEND. This is free legal advice and the author of such advice is not even certified to give it out, so by continuing to read this, you are agreeing to take full responsibility for your own actions and tweets.

- Follow people who are funny, smart, interesting, and thought provoking. Watch and learn from them. Study their writing style, the types of information they tweet, and the frequency.

Twapter 8

Let's Find Some Peeps to Tweet

Twapter 8: Let's Find Some Peeps to Tweet

Most people get it backwards when they start on Twitter. Most focus on how to get thousands of followers. At least once a day I see a tweet that asks, "Do you want to get 80,000 followers in the next 2 days?" Instead, newbie tweeters should focus on how to find great people to learn from and follow. The followers will come if you have built your nest right—photo, bio, first few tweets.

The FIND PEOPLE tab on Twitter will help you find people by name or keyword, if that word is in their profile name. (*figure* 8.1) If you are looking for Bob Barker, type his name in the SEARCH field, and it will pull all accounts that have Bob Barker in the account name. This search feature does not pull keywords that people are tweeting about, but it can help you find some of your favorite people to follow.

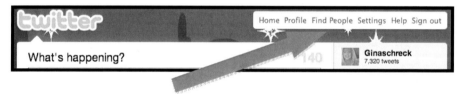

Figure 8.1

You can also use the Twitter keyword search in the middle of the right side bar. (*figure* 8.2) Simply enter a word or phrase and it will pull folks who are tweeting about that topic. You can see if there are folks who look interesting to follow or retweet.

Figure 8.2

There are also sites like www.search.twitter.com. (*figure* 8.3) On this site you can type in keywords that interest you. This will bring up people who are tweeting these words and you can scan for people to follow.

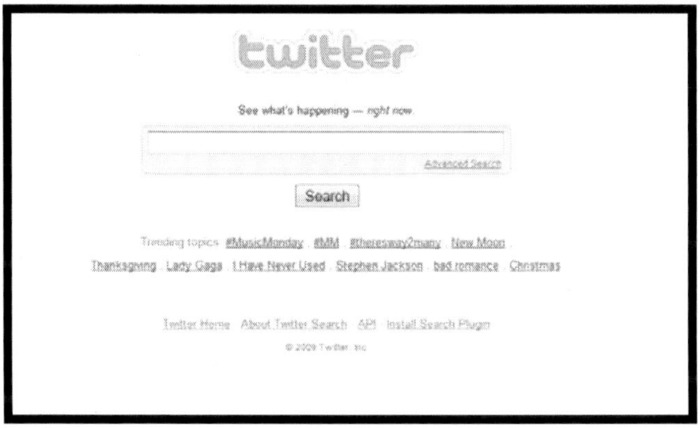

Figure 8.3

There are many directories such as **Twellow** that allow you to search categories or industries for new peeps to tweet. (www.Twellow.com) Twellow has a local feature which they call Twellowhood, if you are trying to build a local following.

Mr. Tweet (www.MrTweet.com) is a nice site that is built around recommendations. You can go there to simply find people in your industry to follow, and Mr. Tweet will make fine recommendations based on the keywords you use, or you can recommend your fellow tweeters. When you make a recommendation, a message will be tweeted telling the world that you recommend that person and they are likely to reciprocate. The more recommendations you receive, the more Mr. Tweet recommends you to others, so it is a nice circle of Twitter love.

I like the fact that Mr. Tweet recommends people to you based on who has retweeted them, who else in your circle is following them, and then gives stats such as how many people they are following and how many they follow back. Mr. Tweet also provides a ratio on how many they follow back to how many they are following. This gives you an idea of whether they will follow you back or just send out information you may like.

When you click on your own profile through Mr. Tweet, it gives some fun statistics on you. You can see your average tweets per day, the ratio in which you reply to other tweeters, the percentage of your tweets that have links in them and your follower/following ratio. (*figure* 8.4)

Figure 8.4

Another easy-to-use directory is **Tweet Trail** www.TweetTrail.com.
Type in a keyword or location and Tweet Trail will show you the top 20
Twitterers for that category.

TwittGeek www.TwittGeek.com is a great tool to quickly find and add
up to 200 new connections in a day. This is the maximum number
they allow you to follow each day from this site using the FREE service.
The downside to using TwittGeek is you must trust the TwittGeek
robots to select the peeps. I would rather be very selective and
connect with people who are in my industry or those who are
sending out very smart information, so you should use this service with
caution.

You can try it with a very narrow and targeted keyword or phrase in
quotations. Example: Telling TwittGeek to find and follow up to 200
people who use the words "immersive learning" will net me much
better results than if I ask to connect with people using the word
"learning," because there are too many people who might tweet
using that word who are not in my area of expertise.

Just Tweet It www.JustTweetit.com is another directory to help you
make relevant connections with other twitterers.

TweetFind www.TweetFind.com helps us find people and get listed in your interest categories.

TWITin www.Buzzom.com is one tool available on Buzzom's site. This tool will show you who is following you that you are not following back, or who you are following that has not reciprocated. TWITin also recommends 40-50 people and you can follow them straight from that site.

Friend or Follow www.Friendorfollow.com is an interesting site that places your Twitter peeps into three categories: Following, Fans, and Friends.

The FOLLOWING category shows all the folks you are following who are not following you back. This is a great tab to check every so often to clean house, since there will be several people here who followed you at one time, you followed them back, and now they have dropped you for whatever reason. You can click on their profile and unfollow if they are not providing value to your Twitter stream.

The FANS category shows those who are following you but you have not followed them back. FANS lets you check out new folks and perhaps add them to your flock. You may have intentionally not followed them back, but many times you will find those you have overlooked.

The FRIENDS category shows the people you are mutually following. It's all flowers and lollipops here!

Other Places to Find Good Peeps

Look at the conversations your friends or contacts are having with others. If they are witty and informing, click on @theirname. It is a live link that allows you to preview their profile and see if you want to follow them.

There is a trend to send out recommended people to follow on Friday's. Look for tweets on Friday that have the tag, "#FollowFriday" or "#FF" in them with lots of names of recommended peeps. (*figure 8.5*) If you enjoy the tweets coming from the person who is recommending these folks, take off and go examine their profiles and follow them.

Figure 8.5

Don't forget to check out the people who follow you. When you are notified that someone new is following you, or when you click on FOLLOWERS, you will see who is currently following you (*figure* 8.6). You will see their last tweet under their name, which may or may not give you enough information to help you decide whether or not to follow them back. I recommend that you check these people out before hitting FOLLOW.

Figure 8.6

Remember the criteria mentioned in **Twapter 2** regarding setting up your nest? You may want to go to a new follower's profile to see if he has any interesting tweets posted, if his bio is intriguing, and if he is dressed in the photo. If the new follower passes your standards, click the FOLLOW button and add him/her.

A couple of other helpful directories or services that will point you to new peeps to follow are:

Twitter Grader www.Twittergrader.com This site gives you lots of great information along with pointing you to some new peeps to tweet!

Twitterholic www.Twitterholic.com which lets you search more specifically for top twitterers in your city or state **Local Tweeps** www.localtweeps.com allows you to enter your zip code, or any other zip code, to find new peeps in that zone.

Nearby Tweets www.NearByTweets.com lets you put in your zip code and find people tweeting in your neighborhood.

GeoFollow www.Geofollow.com Geo (location based) twitter user search.

LocaFollow www.locafollow.com A Twitter search engine that enables you to **locate and follow** Twitter users by searching in their **Bio** and **Location** fields.

Twibes www.Twibes.com List yourself in your industry groups. Find people with similar interests.

Tweeple411 www.TWeeple411.com Find people with similar interests to follow or add your Twitter or FriendFeed page.

TweetsLounge www.TweetsLounge.com A Yelp style Twitter directory of neighborhood businesses using Twitter. Find a business you like who is using Twitter or list a business here.

Twinester www.Twinester.com Create or join groups and communities for Twitter.

Twitter-Athletes www.Twitter-Athletes.com A directory of verified professional athletes on Twitter. (NFL, NBA, MLB, NHL, Soccer, Golf,

Tennis, MMA, etc.

Zellr www.Zellr.com Directory that will list your Twitter profile with facebook, twitpic, rss, digg and other accounts in a single profile.

Twitter Tip: Once a month, spend one hour going to each of these sites to find new people with whom to connect. Be strategic and look for people who are in your target audience using your keywords. You will soon have a custom nest filled with wonderful Twitter friends and potential customers.

Twapter 9

Follow These Bots Too

Twapter 9: Follow These Bots Too

Aside from people on Twitter, you will find many applications or automated Twitter accounts that provide some useful (and some not-so-useful) information. These automated accounts are called Twitter bots.

To gain the benefit from some of the bots, you must turn on the notification in your settings to send you an email when you receive a direct message (DM) so you do not have to be on Twitter to get the notices. (See **Twapter 2** under *Keeping You Informed*.)

Here are a few Twitter bots that I have used and found at least somewhat helpful:

@Gcal – www.Twitter.com/gcal

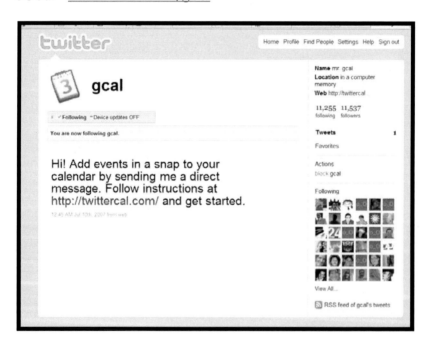

This first bot is one of my favorites for those who use Google calendar. There are 4 simple steps to get this bot working for you:

1. Register at www.Twittercal.com
2. Add @Gcal as a friend on Twitter
3. Grant access to your Google calendar account (steps are on the www.Twittercal.com site)
4. Send your calendar events to @Gcal in a direct message format

---

d gcal meeting with Kelly tomorrow at 9am

d gcal Carpool on Tuesday, 7th of Sept at 7am

@Forecast – www.Twitter.com/Forecast

@Forecast is helpful if you want to know what the weather will be in your area. You simply send a direct message (DM) to @Forecast to find out.

You must first FOLLOW the Forecast Twitter bot and it will follow you back. You must do this first step so that you are able to exchange direct messages. (Remember, you cannot send a person a direct message unless he/she is following you.)

Now when you want your forecast, send the message with the city and state or zip code of the area you would like to know about. The message would read: (see *figure* 9.1)

D Forecast 80125
or
D Forecast Littleton, CO

Figure 9.1

@Timer– www.Twitter.com/Timer

This is a helpful bot that will send you a direct message to remind you of tasks or appointments that you may otherwise forget. @Timer will notify you via direct message on Twitter.

You must first FOLLOW the Timer Twitter bot and it will immediately follow you back, so that you are able to exchange direct messages.

To set the "timer," send a direct message with the number of minutes after which you want to be reminded, followed by the short message you want sent back to you.

WARNING: I have found @Timer not to be extremely punctual (I know, not a good quality for a timer) so do not rely on this if your appointment is very important. It may be a few minutes early or late—This bot seems to take extended breaks at times and may miss the appointment by a couple of minutes.

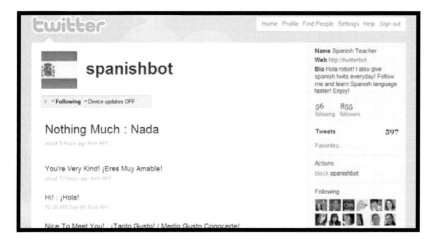

@SpanishBot – www.Twitter.com/Spanishbot

Want to learn Spanish phrases and words? Follow @Spanishbot and learn with each tweet.

@imdb – www.Twitter.com/imdb

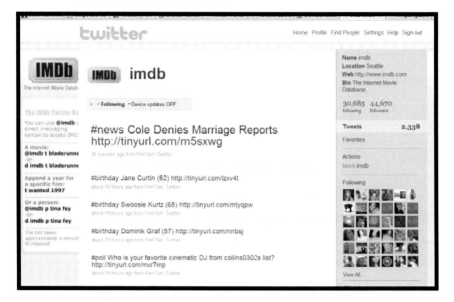

This bot is for movie buffs everywhere. An extension of the popular Internet Movie Data Base site www.imdb.com, the Twitter bot provides information on movies and pop culture. Not only does it respond to direct messages (DM), but @imdb will reply to replies as well. This bot will also send out regular updates with movie trivia and fun quotes.

To utilize this bot, first follow it, and like the others, it will follow you back. Then you can send a request in the form of a Twitter message using these codes:

T – movie trivia and information (add year if needed)
P – movie personality information

So if you want to know when the Wizard of Oz was made, or what it was about and who starred in it, you would type:

> D imdb t Wizard of Oz

or

```
@imdb t Wizard of Oz
```

In less than one minute, (this bot isn't taking popcorn breaks) you would receive a direct message back that reads:

If you wanted information on a celebrity such as Goldie Hawn, type:

```
D imdb p Goldie Hawn
```

or

```
@imdb p Goldie Hawn
```

And very shortly you would have this response:

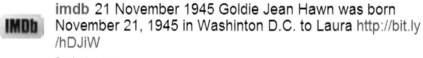

For the book lovers out there, rest assured you can get all the information you want on books and other media from this bot featured by Amazon.

@Junglebot – www.Twitter.com/junglebot

Simply follow @Junglebot and then when you send your request via direct message, you will let the bot know whether you want information on a book, DVD, or music.

```
D Junglebot book Outliers
```

```
D Junglebot music Yanni Voices
```

@Junglebot will send you information on the products from Amazon's
database.

Keep a list of other bots as you encounter them:

_____

_____

_____

_____

_____

_____

_____

_____

_____

_____

_____

_____

_____

_____

_____

_____

_____

_____

_____

_____

_____

_____

Twapter 10

Playing Favorites: Creating Lists & Saving Tweets

Twapter 10: Playing Favorites: Creating Lists & Saving Tweets

One of the newer features on Twitter is the ability to create and follow "Lists." The list feature allows you to create a grouping, or topic of interest, and then add people to these lists whether you are following them or not. You may want to have a list of people you work with or peeps from your city. Or perhaps you want a list of alpaca wool quilters who tweet about their quilts and the adventures of sheering alpacas in the fall. You may not want all of their tweets filling your regular Twitter stream, so a list could be a good place to "store them" until you are ready to quilt. You can create a list for each of your interests or you can find existing lists that have been created by someone else and follow that same list. An existing list is like a frozen dinner—someone has already done the work for you and all you have to do is enjoy.

To create your own lists, simply click on the LISTS link that is on the right of your home page, just under the SEARCH box. (*figure* 10.1) Here you will create a NEW LIST or, once you have a list or two, you will have the option to VIEW ALL of your lists.

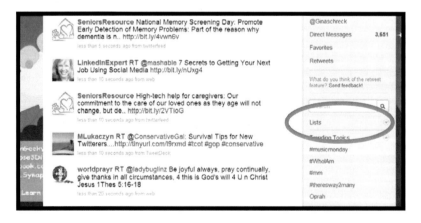

Figure 10.1

Either go through all of your Twitter followers and put select people in your lists, or you can do this as you begin to follow someone or read an interesting tweet from someone. Simply add new people to a list from their profile page. (*figure* 10.2)

Figure 10.2

To follow someone else's lists, go to the profile of someone you follow, click on the follow button and the list will be added to your lists. Check out my lists at www.Twitter.com/Ginaschreck and see the lists I have created.

To find additional lists you can check out Listorious, http://listorious.com, which is a Twitter list directory of the Top 140 Lists.

It's always fun to find out who has you on a list and how they have you categorized. I can guarantee that you will not find me on that alpaca wool knitters list! To see who has you on a list, look for the number that is to the right of your "FOLLOWING" or "FOLLOWERS" numbers. (*figure* 10.3) Click on LISTED.

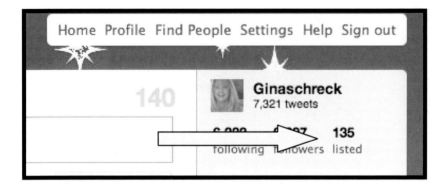

Figure 10.3

Lists are great for your favorite twitterers, but what about those individual tweets? You can mark and collect favorite posts by adding them to your "Favorites" list on your home page. (*figure* 10.4)

Anytime you are reading a tweet that you want to save for later or to just collect for others to see what some of your favorites are, click on the star that appears to the right of the post. (*figure* 10.4) It will fill in solid gold after it is selected.

Figure 10.4

This puts the tweet into your FAVORITES list which can be accessed on the right column under your Direct Messages. *(figure 10.5)*

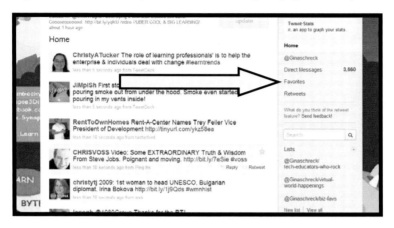

Figure 10.5

Twapter 11

Unfollowing: How & Why to Vote Someone Off Your Tree Branch

Twapter 11: Unfollowing: How & Why to Vote Someone Off Your Tree Branch

It is a good idea to prune your Twitter tree branches regularly (perhaps once a month or so) and give some folks the ol' Twitter boot. Your reasons may differ from mine, but here are a few reasons I unfollow someone and how to do it.

1. **The Dirty Beak!** If someone uses a lot of profanity or tweets about their offensive activities, I will wash their little beaks out with soap and unfollow them! I keep my twitter page rated G or PG. You break that rating rule, you will be unfollowed.

2. **The Hyper-active but Extremely Useless Tweeter.** If someone sends out hundreds of tweets a day blathering on about the color socks they are wearing to the grocery store or the fact that they are now chewing a piece of celery, before drinking another glass of water, they are putting themselves on my endangered Twitterer list. Now personal tweeting is not a bad thing, as long as it is mixed with business or helpful tweets. And there are times when excessive tweeting is tolerated—such as a conference Twitterer—this is where someone is sending out regular tweets from a conference, and I enjoy this since I feel as if I am right there getting information.

3. **The Spammer Sales Tweeter.** This one is obvious. Twitter is a SOCIAL media tool. It is for conversations and sharing, not for pushing your products and services down everyone's beaks. When you look at someone's profile and see that all they tweet is "MAKE MAD CASH ON TWITTER," get them out of there!

4. **The Pump and Dumper.** It took me a while to figure out this one, but there are people who follow hundreds of folks, expecting that they will get most of them following back. After a day or two, they go back and unfollow everyone to make it look as if lots of folks are following them. It keeps their numbers from being too inflated on the "followings" side-something the folks at Twitter frown upon. It is a strange way

to spend time, but many spammers have a goal to have lots of people getting their junk, and because Twitter gets suspicious of someone following thousands of peeps when no one is following them back, the spammers have to keep dumping folks.

I learned about this scam, when I got a message that some new chap was now following my updates. I clicked FOLLOW and the next day when I went to send a personal message thanking him for connecting with me, I noticed the MESSAGE button was not highlighted. (*figure* 11.1) I couldn't understand why I could not see the MESSAGE button and thought there was something wrong with my system or my Twitter account.

Name Richard Branson
Location Probably on Necker Island, my
Web http://fakerichar...
Bio Virgin visionary. Saviour of consumers.

10   47,721   190
following   followers   listed

Tweets   55

Favorites

Actions
block sirdickbranson
report for spam

Following

RSS feed of
sirdickbranson's tweets

Figure 11.1

Important note: If you do not see the word "MESSAGE" in the ACTIONS area, the person is **NOT** following you.

If someone is not following you, you **cannot** send him a **direct message** (DM). Any message you send him is also going out for all of your contacts to see. Use caution. Choose your words carefully, or better yet, just UNFOLLOW him and move on. As my husband always tells me, "Don't let them rent space in your head!"

How do you UNFOLLOW someone? There are a few ways to unfollow a boring, annoying or otherwise undesirable tweeter. The first way is to go to the twit's profile and click the UNFOLLOW button under the photo.

The second method is from your home page. Click on the FOLLOWERS link in the top right column. Now scroll through your followers, find the twit, and select UNFOLLOW. This is a bit more difficult when you have lots of followers.

The third method involves using your third-party management tool such as TweetDeck (Have I mentioned that I love TweetDeck?) Click on the bottom right corner of the person's picture. Select USER and then UNFOLLOW. (*figure* 11.2)

Figure 11.2

NOTE: Since Twitter does not notify you when someone stops following you, you can use a few tools that will let you know who has kicked you off of their branch in case you want to do some pruning yourself.

There is a helpful website dedicated to notifying you when someone stops following you and displays the last tweet you posted before they dropped you. It is cleverly called QWITTER. http://useqwitter.com

You can also go to FRIEND OR FOLLOW http://friendorfollow.com to see peeps you are following who are not following you. You will find folks there that were following you at one time but have now cut you off their tree. After logging in with your Twitter username, select FOLLOWING to see those who are not reciprocating.

Twapter 12

Setting a No Fly Zone-- How & Why You May Want to Block Someone!

Twapter 12: Setting a No Fly Zone—How & Why You May Want to Block Someone

The first year I was on Twitter, I had only blocked only one person, and that was a creepy guy who sent me messages claiming he was a famous Brazilian actor who wanted to meet with me in New York when he saw that I was there at a convention. Now that Twitter has gained popularity and the sleaze companies have started to flood the twit-stream, I am a blocking machine.

NOTE: Unfortunately, pornography sites are early technology adopters and they have already polluted the Twitter stream. Not only do I NOT want their info, but I also don't want my profile photo or info showing up as one of the peeps they are following. I now happily block many sleazy tweeters.

Now I realize that you can't be in the public using tools like Twitter and Facebook and be completely safe from creepers, but I also know that when your gut tells you to block someone, do it!

I speak and attend many conferences and tweet about them before and during, but I am very careful to never put where I am staying, or where I am going to eat, etc. However, when I am in a group and am trying to round up more peeps at conferences and meetings, I will carefully give out more info.

I know there is a risk in having an online presence. There is just as much risk in being on Facebook, Twitter, YouTube, etc., as there is in speaking at a conference, doing a training program for a group, walking into the grocery store or post office, eating some of my cooking, or wearing four-inch heels! You must exercise caution when doing any of these, but you cannot live in fear either. So when in doubt... BLOCK THEM OUT!

When you feel that someone has made inappropriate comments or is asking for personal information that makes you uncomfortable, you can UNFOLLOW—if you were following him or her in the first place—and then BLOCK. Remember, **these are two different actions.** UNFOLLOW will prevent YOU from receiving any of THAT PERSON'S updates, but BLOCKING will prevent THAT PERSON from seeing YOUR updates. That person will not be able to send a direct message, connect with you again, and will not receive any of your tweets, unless you forgive him or her and take off the block curse and follow them first.

HOWEVER, The person you have unfollowed and blocked can go to your main Twitter page using the direct URL www.Twitter.com/yourname to see your posts. **If you feel that you are in danger, call the police. Sadly, you must not take these kinds of things lightly.**

But let's just say you have an annoying person who seems to always reply with nasty comments to your posts or someone you feel is just getting a little too creepy and you want to block him or her. Take these three simple steps:

1. Go to the person's profile page
2. Click on BLOCK in the sidebar under ACTIONS (*figure* 12.1)
3. You will now notice the word BLOCKED under their photo (*figure* 12.2)

Figure 12.1

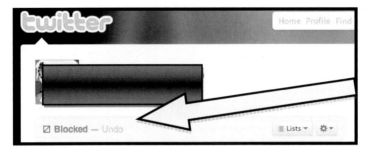

Figure 12.2

Blocking people does not send them a message letting them know they've been blocked, but the next time they try to contact you through direct message or even a reply, they will be notified of the blockage. They will also be prevented from trying to re-follow you.

Should you kiss and make up with the person and want to reinstate them to good Twitter graces, you can simply go to their profile page and click UNDO in that same area.

NOTES on TWITTER APPS:

Twapter 13

The Fine Art of the Hyperlink- Twits of a Feather Link Together

Twapter 13: The Fine Art of the Hyperlink—Twits of a Feather Link Together

Hyperlinks are very important in Twitter Town. If you write a blog post and want to tell the world about it, you can give a quick sentence about the subject to peak interest and then add the link for people to check it out. If you read a great article, watch a helpful or funny video or want to share a website with your tweeps, add the link to your tweet. Remember, in Twitter Town, it's about being a helpful resource—someone who provides great content—even if it is not your own, so add links occasionally to provide value.

NOTE: If you provide a link to a video, it's helpful to tell mention how long the clip is. **Example: Funny 3.5 min vid showing what will happen when we can't make time to read 140 characters:**
http://www.youtube.com/watch?v=BeLZCy-_m3s)

I hate when I click on the video link and find that it is a 30-minute clip I don't have time to watch. Then I have to save the tweet in my favorites to go back later and watch…which I usually don't.

The key is to make it a live link. A link beginning with **http://** makes it live or "clickable" in Twitter. If a link is not clickable, people most likely will not take the time to copy and paste it into a browser. The goal—make it easy, quick, and clickable.

EXAMPLE:

> Finally got the conference recap written up—check it out and add your comments: www.blogs.synapse3Di.com

While this link is live in an e-book format or in an email, it is not live on Twitter and will not be clickable.

> Finally got the conference recap written up—check it out and add your comments: http://blogs.synapse3Di.com

This link will be clickable and folks can go right there and read it.

If you are worried that a link could use up all of your precious 140 characters, stay tuned. In the next Twapter, you will learn about link shrinkers!

Twapter 14

URL Shorteners: Twimming the Wings of a long link

Twapter 14: URL Shorteners: Trimming the Wings of a Long Link

Most links are long and can take up all your character space if you add them without shortening the link first. After all you only have 140 characters available to use and many links are over 50 characters on their own.

To shorten a link for Twitter, Facebook, LinkedIn, and even for use in email, you can go to one of many sites such as: www.tinyURL.com. Simply copy the long URL from the browser and paste it on the site to get your tiny URL.

EXAMPLE:

LONG:
http://www.google.com/search?q=how+to+send+fan+page+invites+to+email+list&ie=utf-8&oe=utf-8&aq=t&rls=org.mozilla:en-US:official&client=firefox-a

This has a length of 144 characters and resulted in the following TinyURL which has a length of 26 characters:

SHORT: **http://tinyurl.com/yklz87y**

You can also give your recipients confidence with a preview TinyURL: **http://preview.tinyurl.com/yklz87y** (more characters used).

Another site I like is: www.bitly.com which saves your past links, tracks how many people clicked on the link, and allows you to post to Twitter directly from there. Create an account here to keep a record of all of your links.

www.virl.com This site uploads pictures and shortens URLs for posting on Twitter, Facebook, Digg, Delicious, Blogs and more.

www.ShortURL.com

These link shortening services will not only shorten your link, but they are permanent, so you can use them over and over. Many of the third-party tools such as Tweet Deck, or Seesmic have link-shortening features built right in. You enter the long link under the tweet, click SHORTEN and it cuts it down to under 25 characters before you hit send.

Twapter 15

Tagging the Wings of Your Tweets Using Hashtags

Twapter 15: Tagging the Wings of Your Tweets Using Hashtags

Grouping tweets for conferences, trending topics, or for other purposes is easily done on Twitter using "hashtags." Hashtags (#), or the "pound sign," mark or identify a tweet as part of a grouping of other tweets. You will see these sprinkled throughout Twitter Town. (*figure* 15.1)

At a conference, someone will usually create a tag that folks can use to mark all tweets referencing information about that conference.

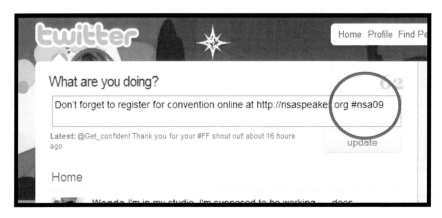

Figure 15.1

Now anyone who searches for that tag will find all tweets from twitterers who have something to say about that conference (as long as they tagged the tweets with the same tag). I do not have to be connected with the folks who are using that tag to still find their tweets. The hashtags pull the groupings of tweets together for me.

During a conference, folks can find out where others are meeting for dinner, which sessions are most helpful, and great quotes and links shared in sessions. Some presenters are even using separate tags for their sessions and having audience members tweet questions and comments about the session and they will have that displayed for all to see. Very cool use of the backchannel that is going on any way. This is also a great way to allow folks who could not attend the conference to feel included and participate with their own questions and comments being displayed.

At conferences you can also use the hashtag to alert audience members of sudden changes or special information that needs to get circulated. The Twitter community becomes your messengers.

Aside from live conferences, hashtags are also used for virtual Twitter meetings and just related topics. For example, each week (Tuesdays from 8pm-10pm ET) the agricultural community gathers to tweet on a specific topic and you will see #agchat on their tweets. Each Thursday night (8pm–10pm ET) there is a large group of educators that get on Twitter with a topic that is chosen ahead of time and they start discussing and sharing information. It's called the Learn Chat session, and their educational, techno-savvy tweets will be tagged with #Lrnchat.

You will frequently see evening tweets tagged with #gno and this is a global group of women gathering for virtual Girl's Night Out. Always fun!

When you see a tweet with a tag in it, you can simply click on the tag and it will show you folks using that tag. You can join in the conversation or just stand on the sidelines and listen. This is another great way to meet interesting people in Twitter Town.

There are some fabulous tools to pull common or trending tweets together. Check out these tools:

1. Go to http://Tweetchat.com and log in with your Twitter name and when it asks which hashtag you would like to follow, type in the tag. This will allow you to send tweets right from here. (figure 15.2) You do not need to put the # sign. You are placed in a "room" where all tweets with your tag will be displayed in one stream. This is a great way to find new folks to connect with too. This is my favorite tool to use when attending a conference or event because you can tweet straight from here without having to remember to add that particular hashtag to each tweet.

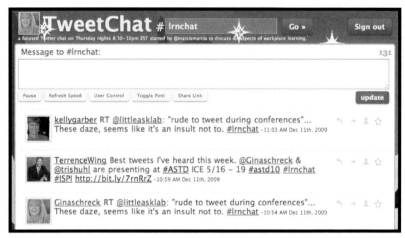

Figure 15.2

You can also be a voyeur here and just type the tag without logging in to read the tweets from folks using it. (*figure* 15.3) This site does not keep an archive of the conference stream like http://search.twitter.com does (See next resource.)

Figure 15.3

2. Go to http://search.twitter.com and type your tag into the SEARCH box to see the twitter feed going on for that tag. You

cannot tweet from here; you can only read others' tweets. From this site you can type in any keyword to see who is tweeting about it. This is a great archive, since it will pull all tweets that have been posted using that particular tag.

3. You can also use http://slandr.net during events form your mobile device. Simply login, click on SEARCH, then enter the tag you want to participate in or watch.

4. Twubs will aggregate your tweets at http://twubs.com. This one incorporates tweets, pictures, and videos in an easy-to-follow format. Like TweetChat, you can also send tweets straight from this site once logged in.

5. A fun (but somewhat ADD-inducing) site for conference use is http://wiffiti.com. This site is fabulous for projecting the tweet stream, or in this case, the tweet-storm in a swirling colorful cloud. Very cool. You can even create a custom background to add a personal touch. I like this tool for conference use.

6. A great conference or event tool to use in hallway screens or to have projected before sessions, during breaks, and during lunch is http://visibletweets.com. This tool shows one tweet at a time and it comes fading in, looking like testimonials. Really like this tool as well.

TWITTER TIP: Warn your followers if you will be sending out an unusually high number of tweets. Let them know that you will be tweeting from a conference for the next 3 days and that if they don't want to be enlightened by your nuggets of knowledge, they can simply ignore you, or go to @Muuter (www.Muuter.com) to "silence" you for a period of time.

NOTES on TWITTER APPS:

Twapter 16

Third Party Tools to Manage the Flock

Twapter 16: Third Party Tools to Manage the Flock

Because the Twitter stream does not stop or wait for you to log on and read the tweets of your favorite peeps, it will seem overwhelming when you do try to sort through them all, even after connecting with a few people. I can remember thinking, "Do I have to stay logged on 24/7 so I don't miss the information that I want to take in?" So imagine how powerful the stream of information becomes when you are connected with 500, 1,000, or 5,000 people! Now throw in Facebook profile updates, Fan Page posts, and LinkedIn. How will you get any other work done?

It's like your never-ending stream of email messages. If you were receiving email from 1,000 people per day, each sending 5-25 messages per day, you would snap. You would need a tool that helps to sort and pull the important messages or those that you really want to read.

Believe it or not there are folks who manage multiple Twitter accounts. So they have several fast moving streams or raging rivers to manage. If you are new to Twitter, you are probably wondering why in the world would anyone want to have more than one Twitter account and how do they manage the madness. If you have several business units within one company or if you are an entrepreneur with a few different businesses running, you just may want to have a Twitter feed for each of them.

I have a separate Twitter account for my cranky dog, Bob. I used to write a weekly column called ASK BOB, where I answered relationship and workplace conflict questions from the voice of our old dog, Bob Barker. I have since moved the column to a Twitter account for him, and you can see some of his replies at www.Twitter.com/BobABarker. Of course his goal is to sell his book, **Ask Bob**, which is coming out soon.

So let's use the Twitter stream analogy. Your stream of information starts small and manageable, but quickly turns into raging waters with more information pouring your way than you can handle.

Now imagine that we take this big stream and start to carve small inlets for your favorite tweets to pool and stay there until you have time to log in and read them. Carve out one for your favorite business peeps; one for your clients who are on Twitter; one for anyone talking about your industry keywords or trends, another pool for your Facebook updates, and one for LinkedIn. You will also carve out a small pool for anyone sending messages directly to you. Once these are set up, you simply open your application, or viewer, and look into the small pools of meaningful tweets while the others in the larger Twitter stream just keep on moving. You do not have to log into Twitter.com, or Facebook, or LinkedIn for that matter. These are just a few of the features that will save you lots of time when using **TweetDeck, Seesmic, HootSuite, CoTweet**, or a few other third-party applications.

Each tool touts unique features, but I have found TweetDeck to be my favorite. You will need to evaluate them based on how you will be using Twitter and other social media sites. Each of the tools mentioned are **FREE** (some do have additional features available for a fee). These tools update frequently (sometimes there are several updates in a row when many changes are made), so you will see many new features even by the time this information reaches your hands.

Since I use TweetDeck every day, I will start with this application and then give some of the unique features on the other tools. To get started on TweetDeck go to http://TweetDeck.com and click DOWNLOAD. TweetDeck's mascot is a crow—which is an annoying bird, if you ask me, but try not to let this fact interfere. TweetDeck runs on Adobe Air so you may have to install that as well if you do not already have the full Adobe suite loaded on your system. It works on PC or Mac (I use it on my PC desktop and Mac laptop) and for those with iPhones, you will find a mobile app for your phone as well (more information on mobile apps in **Twapter 18**).

At first glance you may feel that these applications are very large and cumbersome. The big gray "deck" will take up your entire screen but you will find, in time, that you will use every inch of space. (*figure* 16.1) I'm always looking for the "pretty factor" and I have to admit, TweetDeck definitely didn't get any points in the pretty category until I learned to customize my deck with the colors of my choice. (figure 16.2)

Figure 16.1

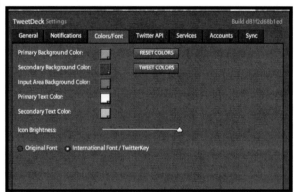

Figure 16.2

The tool starts you off with three default columns, which hardly seem to warrant the size of this tool at first... but just wait, there's more! The first three default columns are: All Friends, Mentions (or Replies), and

Direct Messages. These columns are your "inlets" and you can add as many of these inlets as you'd like. The "All Friends" column is the large Twitter stream in which you will start carving from to reach the other side called sanity. You can move each column left or right and you can add or delete any column individually, so your TweetDeck becomes completely customized.

Managing your corporate or personal brand is always important. You want to know when someone is talking (or tweeting) about you. These tools help you manage your brand easily by having a search column set up with your company name, your competitor's name, or any other keyword you would like to monitor on a regular basis. Just like setting up a "Google Alert" that sends you a notice via email when your name or keyword is used in a blog or elsewhere on the web, TweetDeck, and the other tools, will "alert you" when you or your industry is being tweeted about, and save the tweet in a column for you to read and respond to.

You can also put your peeps into flocks (or groups) such as, "Favorite Biz Peeps," "Colorado Peeps," or even "Beekeepers in Greenland" so you do not have to scroll through thousands of tweets to find those "can't miss" nuggets. TweetDeck has incorporated Twitter's list feature into the deck, so you can create a column for each of the lists that you follow. (More on Twitter lists back in **Twapter 10**.)

Here are some of the other great features that make tweeting so much easier on TweetDeck and some of the other flock management tools.

1. Ability to **FOLLOW** or **UNFOLLOW** someone directly from a search column. You are not necessarily connected with everyone in the search columns. It is pulling their tweets based on the keywords they are tweeting. These can be strangers that you might want to follow and connect with. Hover your cursor over the person's avatar (photo) to see the choices. (*figure* 16.3)

2. Ability to **add a person to a group, view that person's profile, block** him, and even **report that person as a spammer.** If you would like to see more tweets from this person, simply click the **SEARCH** link and TweetDeck will open a column with tweets written by or mentioning the person.

(*figure* 16.3)

Figure 16.3

3. On TweetDeck you can also **REPLY TO ALL** who are mentioned in a tweet, **REFERENCE the link** that was in there for another tweet, and add this tweet to your **FAVORITES.** (See **Twapter 10** for more on favorites.)

4. You can **EMAIL A TWEET** to someone who may not even be on Twitter, straight from TweetDeck. This is a great way to share blog links and other great information that you receive with clients or friends who are still avoiding Twitter Town. (*figure* 16.4)

5. **TRANSLATE** tweets from a foreign language to the language you use in TweetDeck. (*figure* 16.4) This comes in handy when you are working with team members from other countries or if you are connected with interesting tweeters from around the world that speak and tweet in another language. Just click and translate. On TweetDeck you can also translate back, allowing you to type in your native tongue and then select the language to translate into. (*figure* 16.4)

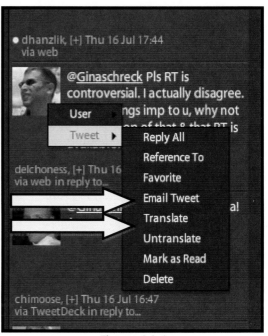

Figure 16.4

6. Worried that you have a link or long URL that will take up your entire 140 characters? TweetDeck (and the others) have built in link shorteners. You can choose to have TweetDeck automatically shorten links by putting a check in the box, **AUTO SHORTEN URL.** (*figure* 16.5) There are times you have a shorter URL or one that you want folks to see, such as when I want to drive viewers to my Getting' Geeky video channel, I want the URL to show as http://GettinGeeky.com and it's not that long. If I auto shorten it will read something like, http://bit.ly/3eNtrE, saving only 2 characters.

Figure 16.5

7. If you get a little wordy when typing your update, you can click the **TWEET SHRINK** button and TweetDeck will magically shrink the update by taking out vowels, changing words like AND with symbols (&), or words like FOR with numbers (4). Pretty amazing feature. (*figure* 16.6)

Figure 16.6

8. TweetDeck and the other power-Twitter tools allow you to **manage multiple Twitter accounts** as well as post updates directly to Facebook (including posting to Fan Pages), LinkedIn, and Myspace. (*figure* 16.7) Follow the three steps on the next page to set this up. This is a fabulous benefit as it will allow you to write a post, decide which of your social media sites you want to post it to and click send. One Stop Tweeting!

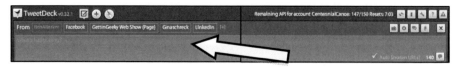

Figure 16.7
STEP 1: This shows which accounts you currently have set up.

STEP 2: Click on the + symbol to open up the account options.

Step 3: Select the type of account you would like to add (Twitter-Facebook-Myspace-LinkedIn) and you may have more than one of each.

NOTE: You will definitely want to customize the settings in TweetDeck. Aside from changing the colors, you will want to turn off the annoying notification sound that makes a robotic tweet noise each time a new tweet comes in. (Although it could be used as a torture device for any co-worker sitting nearby.)

On TweetDeck you can move the pop-up notification window to the bottom or completely off. You can also add other features such as auto-complete username or use narrow columns. Go into your settings and start customizing. (See *figure* 16.8)

Lots of options

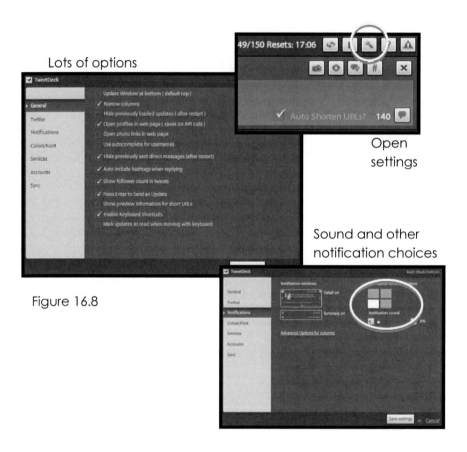

Open settings

Sound and other notification choices

Figure 16.8

Although it many seem as if there is nothing TweetDeck cannot do, I am still waiting for the update that enables it to cook dinner for me, and who knows, as often as they send updates, it might be just around the corner.

Now after spending so much time touting the wonders of TweetDeck, I should give equal billing to Seesmic, Hootsuite and the other competitors...but I'm not going to.

They do offer many of the same features, so I will highlight some areas where they are different. I will point you to the websites to check them out for yourself and see which one suits you best.

Seesmic is the closest competitor to TweetDeck, and there are often blog posts written comparing the two side-by-side. In most user surveys TweetDeck usually wins, but go to www.Seesmic.com and check it out for yourself. (*figure* 16.9)

Figure 16.9

HootSuite is another "Power-Twitter Tool" and can be downloaded at www.hootsuite.com (*figure* 16.10) One of the features that I love about Hootsuite is the statistics that are provided.

Figure 16.10

CoTweet is the power tool for larger corporations using Twitter to engage with customers and manage their company brand. www.CoTweet.com One of its best features is the ability to have multiple people managing up to six Twitter accounts through a single CoTWeet login. (*figure* 16.11)

Another great feature of CoTweet is having the ability to assign tweets to colleagues for follow up. A co-worker can be notified via email that there is a tweet that needs attention. Once they've responded, you'll receive an email containing their response along with the original tweet. (figure 16.12)

Figure 16.11

Figure 16.12

There are many more tools that are a bit simpler to use but if you are planning on using Twitter (along with Facebook and other social platforms), one of these powerhouse apps will meet your needs.

Regardless of the tool you choose, I highly recommend using one of the third-party management tools. It will make your Twitter experience so much more productive and enjoyable. Keep your own list of tools that you encounter along with the features and benefits of each. Feel free to experiment with two or three before making your decision. There is nothing wrong with downloading TweetDeck, using it for a week and then trying Seesmic or Hootsuite each for a week. When you are finished with your evaluation period, simply delete off the programs you are not going to keep. TRY BEFORE YOU BUY...except they are all FREE!

NOTES on TWITTER APPS:

Twapter 17

Managing Your Brand

Twapter 17: Managing Your Brand

Perhaps you jumped on the social media bandwagon to socialize with grade-school chums, look at vacation pictures of total strangers and meet your soul mate. And that's nice...weird, but nice. But let's assume that you spent all this time setting up accounts and learning how to use these social tools to build your business, engage new customers and make more money. Call me crazy, but that is usually the goal for those of us who slave away in cyber-space.

Whether you are in the kayak carving business, coffee bean distribution industry or you are a professional speaker. Whatever the industry, you need to make sure the brand, or image that your business has out in cyber-space is correct and that it is protected.

Gone are the days (hopefully) when we have to spend thousands of dollars on advertising to get people see an image of us that was usually crafted by marketing consultants that we paid to make us look our best. Now it's up to you and me to create that image through content and conversations. Good content and rich conversations.

How do people talk about you when they are in a meeting with their co-workers? When discussing hiring someone to do what you do, does your name come up? This is part of your branding mission. Creating a powerful brand that sticks takes time (or thousands and thousands of dollars) and intention. You must be consistent and focused. Share your expertise on your social media sites, post comments on blogs, write your own blog, collect videos that you have done and those of others that provide helpful information to your potential customers. Be a resource, but all with your brand's "keywords" in mind.

Before we get into HOW to manage your brand, let's take a little detour and spend a few minutes thinking about WHAT you want that brand to be. When your potential customers are searching on-line for you, your products or services, what do they type into the Google search bar? And I don't mean your name. Obviously if they know your name, you won't have to worry about them finding you. But if they are looking for the "best coffee in Denver" or "a web copywriter with sass," or "leadership consultant in Poughkeepsie," does your name come up? Write as many keywords or phrases that describe your business, as you can think of here:

_____

_____

_____

_____

_____

_____

_____

_____

_____

_____

_____

Now these words should be kept somewhere handy for you to look at occasionally as you post information on Twitter, Facebook, LinkedIn or any other social site you are active on. Your videos and photos online should have these words as tags on them. Your Tweets should have them sprinkled in frequently. These words are your branding tools. Now back to our regularly scheduled program...

Twitter has some great features that have made managing your brand easier. Pair that with Google Alerts (www.Google.com/alerts) and your Facebook Fan Page analytic tools, and you become a brand management machine!

It's not enough to measure whether you have thousands of people following your Twitter updates or watching your YouTube videos. You must measure the level of engagement and how others see you in your industry.

On Twitter there are a couple of easy ways to monitor your "brand." First is the SEARCH tool. Type one of your keywords into the search box on the right. If you are using a phrase or two words, be sure and put them in quotations. (*figure* 17.1)

Figure 17.1

This will pull any recent tweets using the exact word or phrase. You can select the green SAVE THIS SEARCH link (*figure* 17.2) and you will be able to monitor this from your Twitter homepage.

Figure 17.2

Another great brand management tool is the list feature (see **Twapter 10**). While this is a fairly new feature, the interesting thing is how it allows you to see how others categorize you. Do they clearly know what you do enough to place you in a list that is labeled with words you would have chosen if you could have named the list? It is an interesting exercise. To see how others "list you" click on the LISTED link (*figure* 17.3)

Ginaschreck
7,444 tweets

147
following   followers   listed

Figure 17.3

Now take a look at the names of LISTS FOLLOWING YOU and see how others see you and the content that you provide. (*figure* 17.4) Could you add more focus to your tweets to have people see you differently? Are you using your keywords so people may actually find your tweet in a Google search? What list do you NOT want to be found in? Be sure to stay out of or minimize Twitter discussions in that arena.

REMEMBER: Each Twitter update is a fully indexed webpage according to Google and other search engines. Your tweet can be found in a search sometimes ahead of your own website!

Although people do want to get to know you and get a glimpse of your personality, be sure and keep your content focused and use words in your tweets (and other social media updates) that your potential customers would be plugging into Google or any other search engine, to find your product or service.

Figure 17.4

Another easy way to monitor your brand, and your name for that matter, is to create a column on TweetDeck (or whichever third-party tool you choose to use) that will pull tweets using specific keywords for your industry and another column for any tweet mentioning your company name. If your name is your brand, like many authors, artists or those in the professional speaking business, be sure to keep a column open that has your name spelled out correctly (different from your @Twittername).

For example I have columns that are always open and monitoring any time someone uses any of these words in a tweet: "Virtual World," "Technology Speaker," "Second Life," "Twitter Speaker," "Gina Schreck," or "Synapse."   This allows me to see if there is someone I should engage in conversation and connect with. If someone were to say something negative about my company or me, it would show up here and I can address the problem before it spread further into Twitter Town and beyond!

Other tools to manage your brand in Twitter Town include:

TweetBeep (www.TweetBeep.com)
TweetScan (www.TweetScan.com)
TwitterAnalyzer (www.TwitterAnalyzer.com)

I also keep Google Alerts set up to notify me if my company, my name, or my very targeted keywords are used elsewhere in cyberspace.

Go to www.Google.com/Alerts and set up the words you want to be notified about. You will receive an email alerting you when these words, or phrases in quotations, are mentioned anywhere on the web—blogs, articles, ezines, and more. Be sure your keywords are very targeted and any group of words, including your name, is typed with quotation marks around them or you will be overloaded with alerts that are not helpful. You may want to tweak the words you monitor if the information you receive is not helpful.

You work hard to build and craft your brand, be sure and protect it. Put in the effort and time upfront and your reward will be thousands of sales people out talking about you and your services...for FREE!

Twapter 18

A Tweet in Your Pocket: Using Your Mobile Device to Stay in Touch with Your Flock

Twapter 18: A Tweet in Your Pocket: Using Your Mobile Device to Stay in Touch with Your Flock

There are some of us who can't wait until we are back at our computers to send out that great nugget of information that we heard at the office party. Or perhaps we are attending a conference and want to share the pearls of wisdom we are gleaning with our tribe of followers, but we didn't bring our laptops. Not to worry. As long as you have a mobile phone handy, you can tweet "on the fly!"

Keep in mind that when you send tweet via text message, using your phones SMS text service, charges may apply. I suggest signing up for an unlimited text plan if you intend to send lots of tweets per month using your phone.

WARNING!

DID YOU KNOW? SMS stands for Simple Message Service which refers to simple text being sent through your cell phone. MMS stands for Multimedia Message Service which is how it is sent when you add a photo or video to a text message!

After connecting your mobile phone in your Twitter set up stage **(Twapter 2)** You will be read to send tweets from your mobile phone. Here are just a few more noteworthy comments about sending messages to Twitter using SMS text messaging.

If you want to send a reply to someone or ensure a specific person on Twitter gets your message, start the tweet with the "@" symbol and then their username. Here is an example:

Compose Message

To: 40404

@ChristinaRampar Will you be leading the group this week at the Second Life meet up? Can't wait to attend.

If you want to send a direct message to someone, it is **CRITICAL** that you start with the letter "D" before the username to ensure it only goes to that person and not to the world. I recently sent a tweet forgetting to start with the D. I wrote, "I'm free tomorrow- call my cell 555-5555." Well you can imagine the grief people gave me when that tweet went out to over 6,000 people! I thought I was going to have to hire a receptionist for the day. Fortunately Twitter Town is filled with wonderfully kind people.

Make sure your message looks like this:

Compose Message

To: 40404

D CarbonBased I'm free tomorrow- call my cell 555-5555.

There are many things you can do from your mobile phone aside from sending updates. Here are a few important commands to remember:

Follow someone new. Perhaps you are at a conference and you meet someone in the halls who tells you she is on Twitter, or you hear the speaker mention that he is on Twitter. You can whip out your phone and type, **"FOLLOW BOBSMITH"** and Twitter will add this person to your friend list. (You do not have to use all capitals. Twitter's commands are not case sensitive and you can use all upper, all lower, or a combination. Type FOLLOW with a space and then the person's Twitter username.)

This is NOT posted to your Twitter timeline and no one will see this message. Twitter is so smart! If you wanted the world to follow Bob Smith you would type "Follow @Bobsmith" and Twitter would know that this message was meant for the world to see.

```
Compose Message

To: 40404

Follow Bobsmith
```

To unfollow someone, go to the website to disconnect from that person. You can type, **"LEAVE Bobsmith"** to no longer follow this person's updates on your phone, but you are still connected with him on your Twitter account.

IMPORTANT: You cannot unfollow someone by typing the word **UNFOLLOW** with their name, so be careful not to send a message out to all of Twitter town saying, **"unfollow Bobsmith,"** or the world will think you are sending out a suggestion to them.

```
Compose Message

To: 40404

Leave Bobsmith
```

Finding out your Twitter stats is as easy as sending an SMS message with the word, **"stats."** You will immediately receive a message from Twitter telling you how many people you are following and how many peeps are following you back.

```
Compose Message

To: 40404

Stats
```

Find out more about a person right from your phone by typing in "WHOIS username". You will receive a message giving you information about when that person started using Twitter, their 160 character bio, their location, and any web link they may have posted in their bio.

Compose Message

To: 40404

WHOIS Saleslounge

Here is what is immediately returned:

Message

From: 40404

Jennifer Abernathy, since Sep 2008. Bio: America's Sales Stylist/Million Dollar Sales Expert. Social Media Speaker/Trainer/Author/Helping others grow their business & brand...Sales Lounge Style!
location: Washing DC Metro
web: http://thesaleslounge.com

Read the most recent tweet posted by someone by typing, **"GET USERNAME"**.

Compose Message

To: 40404

Get COFFEEEMPRESS

NOTE: All of these handy commands can be used on the Twitter website or in the UPDATES box of any third-party tool. Follow the same rules and you will get the same results!

While you can send and receive tweets directly from your cell phone using SMS text messaging, it is so much easier if you can use a tool on your phone that actually has the familiar symbols such as @Replies, DM, favorite a tweet, and even RT, not to mention the fact that if you do not have unlimited text messaging on your mobile phone plan, you could be broke in a month!

If your phone supports mobile applications, you will be able to download the program and tweet all you want without using SMS text.

I will warn you that the ideal client (or app) is hard to find. Many are in beta stage and will have small flaws, but if you keep in mind that this technology is new and created by pioneers, not to mention the fact that most of these are FREE, you will enjoy experimenting with many of them.

I have compiled a list of some of the more popular clients, or apps, that work on today's mobile devices. This is not a complete list and you can find additional resources at the **Twitter Fan Wiki:**

http://twitter.pbworks.com/Apps#Mobileapps

Some are specific to one type of phone and others are open to many mobile devices. Which one is best? Well if you ask 100 people which mobile application is their favorite, you are likely to get at least 75 different answers, so you will have to get out there and try a few for yourself. If you don't like the features, simply uninstall it and try another. I have gone through four or five different clients for my Google Android phone and still feel that there is another, easier to use app just around the corner.

There are new applications created almost daily so by the time you are reading this list, there will be at least a hundred more. These should at least get you started.

iPhone and iPod Touch

- **TweetDeck** has a mobile app for your iPhone or iPod Touch that does almost everything your TweetDeck can do on your desktop. Check it out at www.TweetDeck.com.

- **TweetTime** is a full service Twitter client with a great design for iPhone and ipod Touch users. It is a $0.99 download from the Apple App Store. TweetTime supports multiple accounts, uploads pictures from your camera and library, allows you to post tweets, check others' profiles, and so much more.

- **Twitterrific** has two levels, paid and free. Twitterrific supports multiple Twitter accounts, auto-refresh, and it supports keyboard shortcuts. Twitterrific has the ability to geo-locate and upload photos, all from the entry screen. Some advanced features are only available in the $14.95 version. Find it here: http://iconfactory.com/software/twitterrific

- **Twinkle** is a location aware iPhone and iPod Touch app that allows you to discover and converse with people near to you. Twinkle has the built in ability to upload photos and Twitter status updates. Discover more here: http://tapulous.com/twinkle

Twitter Mobile

Here are a few more resources that you can access on your iPhone and a few other smart phones.

- **PoliticoTracker Twitter Edition** – read any US politician's tweets - plus state-wide feed aggregation. Available through the Apple iPhone apps store.

- **ooTunes Radio** – An iPhone/iTouch app audio player that can tweet what song or radio station you're listening to.

- **Twit Tuner** – This is the app for those who need to know "What's happening right now?" It is available for the iPhone and iTouch and allows you to browse the current top ten Twitter trends.

- **Twittelator Pro** – A best of breed Twitter client for the iPhone and iTouch, Twittelator Pro features myriad features sure to satisfy even the most seasoned of tweeters. Available through the Apple apps store for $4.99 or get more information here: http://www.stone.com/Twittelator

Android

- **Twidroid** – A full-featured client for Android mobile phones. (This is the one I use.) Post tweets, reply to updates, retweet, check someone's profile, read your replies or direct messages, and lots more. This app is free at the Android market. To read more about this great tool check out: http://twidroid.com/features

- **Twitta** – This Android app does a good job of bringing you most of the Twitter features such as posting tweets, checking your direct messages, and @replies. Twitta doesn't support viewing @messages and direct messages as a separate screen. It shows all tweets from your network together. It does support @replies and re-tweeting. It is one of the leanest clients at only 121Kb so it doesn't take much space on your phone. Available through the Android app market. Some additional information here: http://www.androidfreeware.net/download-twitta.html

- **Twoid** – This application has very few options, which may appeal to users who want a simple setup and a simple client. Twoid remembers your login information after the client's initial start. There are very easy-to-use features and functions. Available at the Android market. More information on this app is available here: http://micromedia.cz/iphone-and-android-development

Blackberry

- **TwitterBerry** – TwitterBerry is great and runs on most Blackberry devices. It is free and you can download straight from your phone or go to www.orangetame.com/ota/twitterberry to sign up and have it sent to your phone. Using the menu, you can switch from one screen to another (DM-direct messages, @-Replies or mentions, and all tweets).

- **TinyTwitter** – This is another great mobile client that has a Java version for most Blackberry phones and any other mobile device that supports Java. It is a free application and you can download it from www.TinyTwitter.com . TinyTwitter allows you to read all tweets, @-Replies, and DM-Direct messages sent to you. There are many features that are packed in this TinyTwitter client!

- **Blackbird** – A simple lightweight twitter client for Blackberry smartphones. Because of its stripped down features it is good for newer users who have smaller networks. Download at http://dossy.org/twitter/blackbird.

Any phone

- **Dabr** – Described as "m.twitter.com on steroids." http://dabr.co.uk

- **Trottr** – This app allows you to send audio messages to anybody around the world. All by making a simple phone call. http://Trottr.com

- **Tweete** – Mobile Tweete is a lightweight mobile website. It features user timelines, replies, direct messages, users, favorites. It focuses on being a super-lightweight client. Find out more here: http://m.tweete.net/help

- **Twitizer** – An exciting new service that enables you to send long texts, photos (or other pictures, optionally geotagged), video clips and/or audio clips (or podcasts) from your mobile phone and get them published on Twitter. Check out: http://twitizer.com

- **Twitwoop** - Call a twitwoop number and leave a voice message to your followers. Twitwoop lets you send voice messages to your Twitter timeline and speak a 140 second message! More info at: http://twitwoop.com

- **Twitterfone** is another wonderful application that allows you to call a local number and speak your tweet into the phone. Your message will be converted to text and posted on your Twitter time line. More info at: http://www.twitterfone.com

Other Mobile Apps for Twitter:

Twapter 19

Using a Stwategy to Build Your Business (and save tons of time)

Twapter 19: Using a Stwategy to Build Your Business (and save tons of time)

Hopefully by now you understand the importance of this tool and how to set up your "nest" for success. Let's apply a specific strategy to manage your flock.

If managed correctly, and this includes using a tool such as TweetDeck, Seesmic, HootSuite, or one of the other many Twitter management tools, you will be connecting with people in your target market, engaging those people in stimulating conversations, sharing your expertise, and building a loyal fan base.

Because the stream of conversation is never ending, you can easily be swept away in strong Twitter current. My suggestion to anyone fairly new to using social media tools in their business strategy is to write up a plan and follow it. Here is a suggested plan I give my clients:

1. Create a list of keywords and phrases that your potential customers would type into Google search to find you or your services. Some examples of keywords or phrases might be: "franchisor conferences," "software Instructor," "leadership speaker," "customer service trainer in Boise." Next, make a list on another page of keywords and phrases (known as "long-tail search terms") for your business.

_____

_____

_____

_____

_____

_____

_____

_____

_____

_____

_____

_____

_____

_____

_____

_____

_____

_____

_____

_____

_____

Keep this list somewhere near your computer at least for the first 30 days using this plan, until you become accustomed to incorporating them into your social marketing strategy.

2. Review your list of keywords each day and try to use them one or two times in your Facebook updates, Tweets, LinkedIn updates, and any other place you are putting out information. Remember, your tweets and updates are Google indexed and can be found in a search.

3. Write a list of 10-20 tips that you will send out in the form of updates throughout the week. What can you offer your peeps in the form of expertise or information that will show your value? If you write them ahead of time, you can either schedule them using a tool like www.TweetLater.com or just have something preplanned to send out each day. Go ahead, try it! Make a list of helpful tips that could become some of your first tweets.

_____

_____

_____

_____

_____

_____

_____

_____

_____

_____

_____

_____

_____

_____

_____

_____

_____

_____

4. Spend 30 minutes, each morning, working on a blog post (if you are blogging). This can be editing, writing, adding links, videos, etc. If you do not have a blog of your own yet, spend that 30 minutes reading and commenting on other people's blogs. Find a few favorite blogs and be a regular commenter. Choose a blog where you can show your expertise (without sounding like a jerk, arguing with the writer and other contributors) but definitely don't be afraid to be controversial at times if it is something you have strong feelings about.

5. Spend 30-45 minutes, each morning, scanning and commenting on the updates on your Facebook, LinkedIn, and Twitter accounts. (Comment on any other pages that you are active in as well.)

   Taking time to scan your Facebook home page and commenting on the updates of those with whom you are connected does not mean to spend this time commenting on Aunt Ruth's family picnic photos or your college buddy's love life updates. This means commenting and asking questions that both build your relationships or showcase your professional knowledge base. Save those personal updates for "non-pay time" later in the evening.

6. At the end of each day, scan your social media sites once again, post another tip and reply to any comments made directly to you. This should take approximately 20-30 minutes.

Keep in mind that your goal is to engage people with "social" conversation while they get to know you and like you. Once they like you they will begin buying from you or referring business to you.

Use the sheets on the following pages to track your progress. At least once a week fill in the information and analyze what is working and what needs to be tweaked.

You will notice that I have incorporated Twitter, Facebook, and LinkedIn. Track whichever tools you are using, and at least once a week. This will allow you to see where you should put more effort or where you can spend less time. Through tracking you will discover what works for you and what you need to change.

Social Media Tracking Sheets

Date: _____

Twitter: # Following _____   # Followers _____
Grps listed in _____ Key list topics: _____
_____
Anything noteworthy: _____
_____

Facebook: # Friends _____ # Fans (fanpage) _____
Fan Page Rating: _____ # Interactions: _____
Anything noteworthy: _____
_____

LinkedIn: # Contacts _____ # Recommendations _____
Noteworthy Group Activity: _____
_____
_____

Other: _____
_____
_____
_____

Ideas & Interesting Nuggets to Post: _____
_____
_____
_____
_____
_____
_____
_____

Social Media Tracking Sheets

Date: _____

Twitter: # Following _____   # Followers _____
Grps listed in _____ Key list topics: _____
_____
Anything noteworthy: _____
_____

Facebook: # Friends _____   # Fans (fanpage) _____
Fan Page Rating: _____   # Interactions: _____
Anything noteworthy: _____
_____

LinkedIn: # Contacts _____   # Recommendations _____
Noteworthy Group Activity: _____
_____
_____

Other: _____
_____
_____
_____

Ideas & Interesting Nuggets to Post: _____
_____
_____
_____
_____
_____
_____

Social Media Tracking Sheets

Date: _____

Twitter: # Following _____ # Followers _____
Grps listed in _____ Key list topics: _____

Anything noteworthy: _____
_____

Facebook: # Friends _____ # Fans (fanpage) _____
Fan Page Rating: _____ # Interactions: _____
Anything noteworthy: _____
_____

LinkedIn: # Contacts _____ # Recommendations _____
Noteworthy Group Activity: _____
_____
_____

Other: _____
_____
_____
_____

Ideas & Interesting Nuggets to Post: _____
_____
_____
_____
_____
_____
_____
_____

Social Media Tracking Sheets

Date: _____

Twitter: # Following _____ # Followers _____
Grps listed in _____ Key list topics: _____
_____
Anything noteworthy: _____
_____

Facebook: # Friends _____ # Fans (fanpage) _____
Fan Page Rating: _____ # Interactions: _____
Anything noteworthy: _____
_____

LinkedIn: # Contacts _____ # Recommendations _____
Noteworthy Group Activity: _____
_____
_____

Other: _____
_____
_____
_____

Ideas & Interesting Nuggets to Post: _____
_____
_____
_____
_____
_____
_____
_____

Social Media Tracking Sheets

Date: _____

Twitter: # Following _____   # Followers _____
Grps listed in _____ Key list topics: _____

Anything noteworthy: _____
_____

Facebook: # Friends _____   # Fans (fanpage) _____
Fan Page Rating: _____   # Interactions: _____
Anything noteworthy: _____
_____

LinkedIn: # Contacts _____   # Recommendations _____
Noteworthy Group Activity: _____
_____
_____

Other: _____
_____
_____
_____

Ideas & Interesting Nuggets to Post: _____
_____
_____
_____
_____
_____
_____
_____

Social Media Tracking Sheets

Date: _____

Twitter: # Following _____   # Followers _____
Grps listed in _____ Key list topics: _____
_____
Anything noteworthy: _____
_____

Facebook: # Friends _____   # Fans (fanpage) _____
Fan Page Rating: _____   # Interactions: _____
Anything noteworthy: _____
_____

LinkedIn: # Contacts _____   # Recommendations _____
Noteworthy Group Activity: _____
_____
_____

Other: _____
_____
_____
_____

Ideas & Interesting Nuggets to Post: _____
_____
_____
_____
_____
_____
_____
_____

Social Media Tracking Sheets

Date: _____

Twitter: # Following _____   # Followers _____
Grps listed in _____ Key list topics: _____

Anything noteworthy: _____
_____

Facebook: # Friends _____ # Fans (fanpage) _____
Fan Page Rating: _____ # Interactions: _____
Anything noteworthy: _____
_____

LinkedIn: # Contacts _____   # Recommendations _____
Noteworthy Group Activity: _____
_____
_____

Other: _____
_____
_____
_____

Ideas & Interesting Nuggets to Post: _____
_____
_____
_____
_____
_____
_____
_____

Social Media Tracking Sheets

Date: _____

Twitter: # Following _____ # Followers _____
Grps listed in _____ Key list topics: _____
_____
Anything noteworthy: _____
_____

Facebook: # Friends _____ # Fans (fanpage) _____
Fan Page Rating: _____ # Interactions: _____
Anything noteworthy: _____
_____

LinkedIn: # Contacts _____ # Recommendations _____
Noteworthy Group Activity: _____
_____
_____

Other: _____
_____
_____
_____

Ideas & Interesting Nuggets to Post: _____
_____
_____
_____
_____
_____
_____
_____

Social Media Tracking Sheets

Date: _____

Twitter: # Following _____   # Followers _____
Grps listed in _____ Key list topics: _____

Anything noteworthy: _____
_____

Facebook: # Friends _____   # Fans (fanpage) _____
Fan Page Rating: _____   # Interactions: _____
Anything noteworthy: _____
_____

LinkedIn: # Contacts _____   # Recommendations _____
Noteworthy Group Activity: _____
_____
_____

Other: _____
_____
_____
_____

Ideas & Interesting Nuggets to Post: _____
_____
_____
_____
_____
_____
_____
_____

Social Media Tracking Sheets

Date: _____

Twitter: # Following _____   # Followers _____
Grps listed in _____ Key list topics: _____
_____
Anything noteworthy: _____
_____

Facebook: # Friends _____   # Fans (fanpage) _____
Fan Page Rating: _____   # Interactions: _____
Anything noteworthy: _____
_____

LinkedIn: # Contacts _____   # Recommendations _____
Noteworthy Group Activity: _____
_____
_____

Other: _____
_____
_____
_____

Ideas & Interesting Nuggets to Post: _____
_____
_____
_____
_____
_____
_____
_____

Social Media Tracking Sheets

Date: _____

Twitter: # Following _____   # Followers _____
Grps listed in _____ Key list topics: _____
_____
Anything noteworthy: _____
_____

Facebook: # Friends _____   # Fans (fanpage) _____
Fan Page Rating: _____   # Interactions: _____
Anything noteworthy: _____
_____

LinkedIn: # Contacts _____   # Recommendations _____
Noteworthy Group Activity: _____
_____
_____

Other: _____
_____
_____
_____

Ideas & Interesting Nuggets to Post: _____
_____
_____
_____
_____
_____
_____
_____

Social Media Tracking Sheets

Date: _____

Twitter: # Following _____   # Followers _____
Grps listed in _____ Key list topics: _____
_____
Anything noteworthy: _____
_____

Facebook: # Friends _____   # Fans (fanpage) _____
Fan Page Rating: _____   # Interactions: _____
Anything noteworthy: _____
_____

LinkedIn: # Contacts _____   # Recommendations _____
Noteworthy Group Activity: _____
_____
_____

Other: _____
_____
_____
_____

Ideas & Interesting Nuggets to Post: _____
_____
_____
_____
_____
_____
_____
_____

Social Media Tracking Sheets

Date: _____

Twitter: # Following _____   # Followers _____
Grps listed in _____ Key list topics: _____

Anything noteworthy: _____
_____

Facebook: # Friends _____   # Fans (fanpage) _____
Fan Page Rating: _____   # Interactions: _____
Anything noteworthy: _____
_____

LinkedIn: # Contacts _____   # Recommendations _____
Noteworthy Group Activity: _____
_____
_____

Other: _____
_____
_____
_____

Ideas & Interesting Nuggets to Post: _____
_____
_____
_____
_____
_____
_____
_____

Social Media Tracking Sheets

Date: _____

Twitter: # Following _____   # Followers _____
Grps listed in _____ Key list topics: _____

Anything noteworthy: _____
_____

Facebook: # Friends _____   # Fans (fanpage) _____
Fan Page Rating: _____   # Interactions: _____
Anything noteworthy: _____
_____

LinkedIn: # Contacts _____   # Recommendations _____
Noteworthy Group Activity: _____
_____
_____

Other: _____
_____
_____
_____

Ideas & Interesting Nuggets to Post: _____
_____
_____
_____
_____
_____
_____
_____

Social Media Tracking Sheets

Date: _____

Twitter: # Following _____   # Followers _____
Grps listed in _____ Key list topics: _____

Anything noteworthy: _____
_____

Facebook: # Friends _____   # Fans (fanpage) _____
Fan Page Rating: _____   # Interactions: _____
Anything noteworthy: _____
_____

LinkedIn: # Contacts _____   # Recommendations _____
Noteworthy Group Activity: _____
_____
_____

Other: _____
_____
_____
_____

Ideas & Interesting Nuggets to Post: _____
_____
_____
_____
_____
_____
_____
_____

Social Media Tracking Sheets

Date: _____

Twitter: # Following _____   # Followers _____
Grps listed in _____ Key list topics: _____
_____
Anything noteworthy: _____
_____

Facebook: # Friends _____ # Fans (fanpage) _____
Fan Page Rating: _____   # Interactions: _____
Anything noteworthy: _____
_____

LinkedIn: # Contacts _____ # Recommendations _____
Noteworthy Group Activity: _____
_____
_____

Other: _____
_____
_____
_____

Ideas & Interesting Nuggets to Post: _____
_____
_____
_____
_____
_____
_____
_____

Social Media Tracking Sheets

Date: _____

Twitter: # Following _____   # Followers _____
Grps listed in _____ Key list topics: _____
_____
Anything noteworthy: _____
_____

Facebook: # Friends _____ # Fans (fanpage) _____
Fan Page Rating: _____   # Interactions: _____
Anything noteworthy: _____
_____

LinkedIn: # Contacts _____ # Recommendations _____
Noteworthy Group Activity: _____
_____
_____

Other: _____
_____
_____
_____

Ideas & Interesting Nuggets to Post: _____
_____
_____
_____
_____
_____
_____
_____

Social Media Tracking Sheets

Date: _____

Twitter: # Following _____   # Followers _____
Grps listed in _____ Key list topics: _____
_____
Anything noteworthy: _____
_____

Facebook: # Friends _____ # Fans (fanpage) _____
Fan Page Rating: _____   # Interactions: _____
Anything noteworthy: _____
_____

LinkedIn: # Contacts _____ # Recommendations _____
Noteworthy Group Activity: _____
_____
_____

Other: _____
_____
_____
_____

Ideas & Interesting Nuggets to Post: _____
_____
_____
_____
_____
_____
_____
_____

Social Media Tracking Sheets

Date: _____

Twitter: # Following _____   # Followers _____
Grps listed in _____ Key list topics: _____

Anything noteworthy: _____
_____

Facebook: # Friends _____   # Fans (fanpage) _____
Fan Page Rating: _____   # Interactions: _____
Anything noteworthy: _____
_____

LinkedIn: # Contacts _____   # Recommendations _____
Noteworthy Group Activity: _____
_____
_____

Other: _____
_____
_____
_____

Ideas & Interesting Nuggets to Post: _____
_____
_____
_____
_____
_____
_____
_____

Social Media Tracking Sheets

Date: _____

Twitter: # Following _____   # Followers _____
Grps listed in _____ Key list topics: _____
_____
Anything noteworthy: _____
_____

Facebook: # Friends _____ # Fans (fanpage) _____
Fan Page Rating: _____ # Interactions: _____
Anything noteworthy: _____
_____

LinkedIn: # Contacts _____ # Recommendations _____
Noteworthy Group Activity: _____
_____
_____

Other: _____
_____
_____
_____

Ideas & Interesting Nuggets to Post: _____
_____
_____
_____
_____
_____
_____
_____

Social Media Tracking Sheets

Date: _____

Twitter: # Following _____   # Followers _____
Grps listed in _____ Key list topics: _____
_____
Anything noteworthy: _____
_____

Facebook: # Friends _____ # Fans (fanpage) _____
Fan Page Rating: _____ # Interactions: _____
Anything noteworthy: _____
_____

LinkedIn: # Contacts _____ # Recommendations _____
Noteworthy Group Activity: _____
_____
_____

Other: _____
_____
_____
_____

Ideas & Interesting Nuggets to Post: _____
_____
_____
_____
_____
_____
_____
_____

Extra, Extra!

Twictionary of Twitter Terms

Twictionary of Twitter Terms

Avatar: This is your picture or icon on Twitter (and any other website and social media site). An avatar is simply a digital representation of yourself, as well as a really cool movie.

Badge: The small box, icon, or photo of the Twitter logo or bird that you place on your website, blog, or other sites that links to your Twitter page.

Bird-of-Mouth: News heard in the Twitter stream.

Bot: An automated account that is set up to send you some type of information in response to a specifically formatted message.

Carpal Twunnel Syndrome: The onset of pain in hands from spending too much time on Twitter.

Celebirdie: A famous person from television or the music industry that enters Twitter Town.

Dweet: A tweet sent while under the influence of alcohol. Can also refer to the twit who sent the dweet.

Fail Whale: The adorable whale that appears when Twitter is over-capacity telling you to wait and try logging in a bit later.

Hashtag: A code or word that begins with the hash mark or pound sign (#) to group tweets.

Hypertweeter: A person who posts so many updates in a day that others want to unfollow him, but usually don't because the hypertweeter has good content (see @Scobleizer).

Mistweet: A tweet one later regrets, perhaps because of a dweet.

MMS Text: Multimedia Message Service – a message sent from a cell phone that has a photo or video attached.

Retweet: The act of forwarding a tweet to your followers including the acknowledgement of the originator.

SMS Text: Simple Message Service – a message sent from a cell phone with no photos or media attached.

Snit: A Twitter Snob—also known as a Twob. One who looks down upon the lowly twirgin who's just getting started and trying to figure out the whole twitterverse.

Twackle: Sports related tweets as well as a website with twitterers from the world of sports. http://Twackle.com

Twainer: Someone who teaches others how to use Twitter.

Twapaprazzi: Someone who is obsessed with tweeting about celebrities and Twitterlebrities.

Twarcissist: Someone who tweets incessantly about himself...oh I guess that would be everyone on Twitter!

Twarfing: Spewing out personal information that is more than ANYONE needs to know. Also refers to useless tweet overload.

Twargument: A debate or argument played out on Twitter. Usually started by Twerks!

Twatcher: A person who signs up for Twitter but never tweets or gets involved. They simply watch and listen. (My husband is a total Twatcher!)

Tweeper: Someone who happens to always show up at events you tweet about and knows eerie details about your life that you don't remember tweeting.

Tweeps: Twitter Peeps. Those in your nest or those following your updates. Also known as Peeps.

Tweet: Verb or noun – a question, statement, or sound made by humans on Twitter. Must be 140 characters or fewer of information, questions, or other short rants. Also something you do incessantly once on Twitter!

TweetUp: A live event where your Tweeps gather, usually to tweet in the same room!

Tweetwalking: Walking as you tweet—not easy to do and most tweetwalking leads to twipping.

Twerk: A jerk who loves to start controversy or make nasty remarks to other's tweets. (Twerks soon become Blocked-Twerks!)

Twijacker: Someone who hijacks a hashtag to push his/her product, service, or point-of-view. Highly distasteful and will cause an uprising of angry tweeters!

Twircular Tweet: The phenomenon of a tweet being retweeted so many times that it comes back to the original tweeter; with one difference: the credit has been attributed to some stranger on the other side of the world.

Twird: A jerk, idiot, or turd who writes nasty notes to you just before you block him!

Twirgin: Someone brand new to Twitter before posting the first tweet.

Twirp: This one is self-explanatory! (See also: Twird)

Twitterholic: This is both a person and a website. If you are ready for the 12-step Twitter program and are asking your children to contact you through tweets and you call your spouse "@honey," you are a Twitterholic. You can also go to www.Twitterholic.com to connect with top Twits.

Twitterlebrity: Similar to Celebritwitty, but not necessarily known outside the Twitter community. A Twitterlevrity is someone who has thousands and even millions of followers. A Twitterlebrity can't walk into a grocery store or dry cleaners without someone recognizing him or her. (This may require the Twitterlebrity to hold up his hands as if cropping his head to enable the person to recognize him as the tiny photo seen on the Twitter screen.)

Twoops: Any embarrassing information that was intended as a private message but accidentally goes out to the world. Can also be a half-baked tweet that got sent before its time.

Twoosh: A perfect140 character tweet. Packing it in!

Twouble: What you are in after posting controversial tweets that will certainly cause a commotion.

When Things
Go Wrong

When Things Go Wrong

Here are some of the cute pictures and messages you will encounter occasionally on Twitter. When you see these, you can usually just hit refresh on your browser and all will be well with the world.

This is the dreaded "Fail Whale." There are times when too many beaks are flapping and Twitter can't handle it. When it is overloaded, you will see this cute little whale along with a message telling you they are trying to lighten the load.

You can choose to wait a few minutes, or do like I do, just click refresh over and over until it is back!

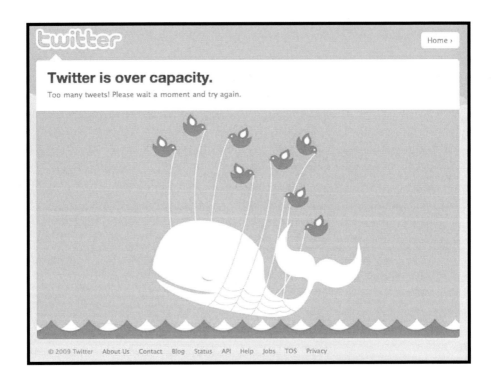

What Others Say About Gina Schreck

"Everyone is still talking about how much information they receive every time you come and talk to our group. You make learning all this new information fun and easy. Can't wait to have you back."
~ **@LizFiddes** – (Education Coordinator, CREA)

"Gina is a great resource for trend watching and all things Geeky!"
~ **@BeyondtheBrink** (Christina Ramparstad- Speaker and Owner of Beyond the Brink Consulting)

"After seeing your presentation previously, I had built you up considerably and you did not disappoint! Everyone was talking about this being the most educational and engaging presentation they had been to. I am a FAN! Great job!"
~ **@Qwert2** -(Tom Knight- Horizon Logistics)

"Thanks for sharing all of your background on social media. Your expertise helped immensely in writing about tweet breach."
~ **@John_Sileo** -(Identity Theft Expert and Author of **Stolen Lives: Identity Theft Prevention Made Simple** and **Privacy Means Profit**)

"I've spent a lot of time and attended other info sessions on this topic, so I was not really sure if I would learn much new from attending this presentation. How wrong I would have been to miss this – Gina is tops in this area and delivered a lot of useful and important information."
~ **William Shepard** (W. J. Shepard Consulting, L.L.C.)

NOTES:

How to Reach Gina Schreck

If you would like to bring in Gina to speak to your group – large conferences or small group consulting – you can reach her, obviously on Twitter: www.Twitter.com/GinaSchreck

or via email: Gina@Synapse3Di.com.

If you are looking for a mailing address, you must be riding in a horse-drawn carriage and like licking stamps, but what are you doing with this book in your possession?

Check out more amazing learning resources at:
www.Synapse3Di.com
www.GettinGeeky.com
www.Facebook.com/GettinGeeky